Q & A: Alcoholism and Sobriety

Hindsfoot Foundation Series on Treatment and Recovery

Q & A: Alcoholism and Sobriety

Jane S.

iUniverse, Inc.
New York Lincoln Shanghai

Q & A: Alcoholism and Sobriety

iUniverse books may be ordered through booksellers or by contacting:

iUniverse
2021 Pine Lake Road, Suite 100
Lincoln, NE 68512
www.iuniverse.com
1-800-Authors (1-800-288-4677)

ISBN-13: 978-0-595-42334-7 (pbk)
ISBN-13: 978-0-595-86672-4 (ebk)
ISBN-10: 0-595-42334-5 (pbk)
ISBN-10: 0-595-86672-7 (ebk)

Printed in the United States of America

For Kay H.

Keep yourself like an empty vessel for God to fill. Keep pouring out yourself to help others so that God can keep filling you up with His spirit.... To be clear, a lake must have an inflow and an outflow.

—*Twenty-Four Hours a Day*, November 2nd

Every man according as he purposeth in his heart, so let him give; not grudgingly, or of necessity, for God loveth a cheerful giver.

—II Corinthians 9:7

Contents

Introduction

This book makes use of this alcoholic's experience of sobriety, along with experience as a counselor and in corrections work, long experience in A.A. service, and research by others, including research learned about through work reported at the Kirk Collections Seminars at Brown University—and, of course, published "inside" literature on alcoholism and sobriety. There is the book *Alcoholics Anonymous* which we call the Big Book—now nearly seventy years old—there is the A.A. book called *Twelve Steps and Twelve Traditions* (the *12 & 12*, first published a little more than fifty years ago)—and there are two books by Marty Mann which I have found very helpful.

Marty's first book, *Primer on Alcoholism*, was published in 1950 and 1958 (second edition); the second, *Marty Mann Answers Your Questions About Drinking and Alcoholism*, was published in 1970, the year I got sober. These two books were not published by or officially affiliated with Alcoholics Anonymous, but Marty was a very famous early A.A. member—her story is in the Big Book under the title "Women Suffer Too"—and in 1944 she founded the National Council on Alcoholism (now the NCADD, the National Council on Alcoholism and Drug Dependence). This public health organization was a powerful force in removing the public stigma from alcoholism in the United States during the years which followed—Marty worked all her life to make sure the general public knew that alcoholism could now be successfully treated.

Here at the beginning of the twenty-first century, I believe there is now a need for a new brief informative volume directed toward sobriety. Most of the basic facts haven't changed in seventy years or fifty or thirty-five; but some surrounding circumstances have.

Roughly, here's the outline for this book. There are six parts after the Introduction. Chapter I is beginning questions, under the heading *What Is Alcoholism?* Chapter II looks at another set of beginning questions, under the heading *What Is Sobriety?* Chapter III is about the heart of the A.A. program, and asks *What Are the Twelve Steps?* Chapter IV is *Where Can I Go for Help?*—it asks "What Is It Like Going to A.A., and What Do I Do There?" but also asks "What Are Other Answers?" Chapter V is my story, *Jane S. in Sobriety*—which should help answer some of the questions—and then Chapter VI covers *Questions on the Manic-Depressive (Bi-Polar) Alcoholic*.

Chapter I. What is Alcoholism? In the first part, we begin with five questions. They are the questions I asked when it was suggested that I had a drinking problem and ought to be going to meetings of Alcoholics Anonymous. (The word "suggested" probably isn't strong enough for what my husband actually said, which was "You go to those meetings or else I'm leaving.") They are (1) *What is alcoholism?* (2) *How do I know if I have it?* (3) *What do I do now?* (4) *Where does alcoholism come from?* And (5) *Are there alcoholic families?*

Chapter II. What Is Sobriety? I may be an alcoholic. What do I do now? What I do now is, I try to get sober. How? We'll take our look at that in Chapter III. First let's ask, *What Is Sobriety?* That is the subject of Chapter II. *Is 'not drinking' the same as sobriety?* The first quality of my sobriety is that my system is free of alcohol and other substances. Once that is accomplished, sobriety is probably best considered as a mindset learned from regular attendance at meetings, from practicing the Twelve Steps, from a close relationship with a sponsor, from regular prayer and meditation, and from "giving it away." The whole section is about the mindset so perhaps we don't need to consider it as a separate heading. So we ask, *Why meetings?* and *What do you mean by practicing the Twelve Steps?* (there's more on this second question in Chapter III). *What's this about a sponsor? About prayer and meditation? About "giving it away"?* The answers to these questions should give us an idea of what sobriety is.

Chapter III. What Are the Twelve Steps? It seems to be pretty generally agreed that the process of mind-change to deal with alcoholism (or overeating or gambling or narcotics) is outlined in a set of Twelve Steps, developed by Bill W., founder of Alcoholics Anonymous. In the third part of the book, we ask about these Twelve Steps, the same Steps used for Narcotics Anonymous, Overeaters Anonymous, Sex and Love Addicts Anonymous, and any number of other groups who have found them helpful in dealing with their problems. We also ask what we're supposed to do with them (yes, *practice them*, but what's that all about?). A lot of what's in Chapter V (and something of what's in Chapter IV) can be used to show what we do with the Twelve Steps—how we "practice them"—in A.A. and "in all our affairs." It won't do any harm to list these steps here, though they're given several times further on in the book.

These are the Twelve Steps: (1) We admitted we were powerless over alcohol—that our lives had become unmanageable, (2) Came to believe that a Power greater than ourselves could restore us to sanity, (3) Made a decision to turn our will and our lives over to the care of God *as we understood Him*, (4) Made a searching and fearless moral inventory of ourselves, (5) Admitted to God, to ourselves, and to another human being the exact nature of our wrongs, (6) Were entirely ready to have God remove all these defects of character, (7) Humbly asked Him to remove our shortcomings, (8) Made a list of all persons we had harmed, and became willing to make amends to them all, (9) Made direct amends to such people wherever possible, except when to do so would injure them or others, (10) Continued to take personal inventory and when we were wrong, promptly admitted it, (11) Sought through prayer and meditation to improve our conscious contact with God *as we understood Him*, praying only for knowledge of His will for us and the power to carry that out, and (12) Having had a spiritual awakening as the result of these steps, we tried to carry this message to alcoholics, and to practice these principles in all our affairs. [Reprinted with permission of Alcoholics Anonymous]

Chapter IV. Where Can I Go for Help? The fourth part of the book isn't very long (and in fact, the whole book isn't very long), but it has some other important questions and answers (so far as I can provide them). Remember, these are not "A.A. Answers"—they're my answers. But they are based on my experience in and with A.A. We ask (and answer) some questions about A.A., but also about other approaches to sobriety. First we ask, *Where can I go for help?* We talk mostly about A.A. and a little about other answers. When we talk about A.A. we try to answer questions about meetings and about A.A. sayings and slogans and about telling our stories in A.A. We try to say how it is that A.A. can work. And we consider some other questions: *(1) How do I recognize alcoholism in someone I love? and what do I do? (2) Do answers that work for adults work for teenagers or younger adults? (3) What happens if we ignore warnings? (4) Is abstinence the only answer?*

Chapter V. My Story: Jane S. in Sobriety. In Chapter V, very simply, I tell my story, "What it was like, what happened, what it's like now"—that's the recognized "formula" for telling your story in Alcoholics Anonymous. The emphasis is on the word *my.* It's not anyone else's experience. Each one of us has his or her own life as an alcoholic, drunk and then sober. My story is just that—*my* story. But I believe it will help answer questions about alcoholism, sobriety, and the Twelve Steps. I've been surprised, in writing it out, just how long it is. You see, when we "tell our story" in Alcoholics Anonymous, we generally speak for somewhere between thirty and fifty minutes, and we tell whatever parts of our story come into our heart and mind at that time. But I've tried to make as full a story as I can, way beyond what I could tell at a meeting, and though it really isn't anywhere near complete, it's remarkable to see it run for fifty pages instead of fifty minutes. Even so, I've tacked another chapter on, which also tells part of my story, the part that covers my being a bi-polar alcoholic. I say "tacked on" but to me it's more than that, and I'm thinking, from all I've read and heard over thirty-five years, it may be more than a tack-on for quite a number of manic depressives who are (or have been diagnosed as) alcoholics, or alcoholics who are (or have been diagnosed as) manic depressive.

Chapter VI. Questions on the Manic-Depressive (Bi-Polar) Alcoholic As the sixth part of the book, there's the chapter that's been waiting to be written for nearly seventy years, the chapter on the Manic-Depressive (Bi-Polar) Alcoholic. I was formally diagnosed as a manic depressive and placed on lithium therapy in July 1972, when I was sober just over a year and a half. Dr. Silkworth said that the manic-depressive type of alcoholic was the least understood by his friends, and that a whole chapter could be written about him (or her). As I said, my chapter in this book is not Dr. Silkworth's chapter, but it is a chapter written out of my life, and maybe it will help.

It's not a very long chapter, but it does tell some of this particular story from the inside. One other point. Although I am an alcoholic, and much of this book could be described as an "alcoholic's eye view," this is not "the view from A.A." Even if I had seventy years of sobriety, instead of half that, I couldn't speak for Alcoholics Anonymous. No individual alcoholic speaks for Alcoholics Anonymous. Now to our beginning questions.

—Jane S.

CHAPTER I

What Is Alcoholism?

We begin with five questions. They are questions I asked when it was suggested that I had a drinking problem and ought to be going to meetings of Alcoholics Anonymous. Actually, you could say they are parts of a single question and you could summarize that single question as, *Am I an alcoholic?* But broken down into five parts, they are (1) *What is alcoholism?* (2) *How do I know if I have "alcoholism"?* (3) *What do I do now?* (4) *Where does alcoholism come from?* And as part of this, (5) *Are there alcoholic families?*

You'll notice I didn't ask, *What is Alcoholics Anonymous? What's A.A.?* I already knew A.A. was something alcoholics went to, and I really didn't want to know more. And I didn't want to go. What I wanted to know was, *Am I an alcoholic?* I didn't exactly have an open mind. I was really looking for evidence that I wasn't an alcoholic. Of course I wanted to know what this alcoholism was. So what is this *alcoholism*?

What is alcoholism?

My own answer is that alcoholism is two things—one we'll call *Alcoholism-1* and one we'll call *Alcoholism-2.* One is a physical difference in people who are or are likely to be alcoholics—a difference that means alcohol does things for them it doesn't do for other people and also that makes them process alcohol differently from other people. This is genetic and it can be described as a genetic disease or predisposition. The other is what people as far back as 1848 called chronic alcoholism, the shakes, the DTs, the sickness of the bums living "on the Bowery" or "on Skid Row" or under the railroad viaducts with overcoats and bottles in bags. That's what people used to mean by alcoholism—that's *all* they used to mean by alcoholism—and that's what we'll call *Alcoholism-1*. It is also called a disease. (I wasn't aware of my own Alcoholism-1 when I came to A.A. because I took tranquillizers for years—mostly valium—which masked the characteristics of Alcoholism-1.) The physical difference between alcoholics and non-alcoholics, what is sometimes called the *predisposition*, we'll call *Alcoholism-2*.

That's my own view, after thirty-five years of study and life experience. What about other people's views? (I mean the views of other people who have studied the question, or who have lived the answer.) Well, as far as those who have studied the question are concerned, alcoholism is described as a disease, as a disease condition, as a "multigenic" disease, as an illness or a sickness (different from a "disease entity"?), occasionally as an allergy (sometimes an allergy mixed with a compulsion), and sometimes people speak of the "disease concept of alcoholism." Bill W. called it a mental obsession and a physical compulsion. And, oh yes, there are terms (used in technical literature and reports) such as "alcohol dependence" and "alcohol abuse"—terms I'd just as soon avoid. (I'd like to avoid them because there seems to be a kind of "disconnect" between the definitions of the terms and recovery from alcoholism.) And then there is the idea that alcoholism is a disease (or "disease condition") where the symptoms become another disease. What all these have in common is that something is out of order in the response of an "alcoholic" to alcohol. (Sometimes it's good—sometimes *not!*)

I probably *should* have asked, *What's a disease?* It turned out I didn't really know. Never, in my wildest imagination, could I have come up with the official (American Medical Association) definition of a disease. A disease is *an involuntary disability, which is the sum of the abnormal phenomena displayed by a group of individuals, by which they differ from the norm, and which places them at a disadvantage in relation to the norm.*

The definition of alcoholism as a disease (AMA) is that *alcoholism is a primary chronic disease with genetic, psycho-social, and environmental factors influencing its development and manifestations. The disease is often progressive and fatal. It is characterized by continuous or periodic impaired control over drinking, preoccupation with ... alcohol, use of alcohol despite adverse conse-quences, and distortions in thinking, most notably denial.* (This is the defini-tion finally approved by the American Society of Addiction Medicine and thus by the American Medical Association, February 3, 1990, and circu-lated by the National Council on Alcoholism and Drug Dependence, for-merly the National Council on Alcoholism.)

This isn't the way I talk, and it isn't the way most people talk, but most people aren't medical doctors writing definitions of diseases. What exactly does this mean? For one thing, if alcoholism is a *primary* disease, that means it isn't the symptom of some other underlying "disease state." (If I'm an alcoholic, it's not because I first caught x-disease or scarlet fever or chicken-pox or y-disease, which then produced my alcoholism; it's because I "caught alcoholism" or, as they used to say, "came down with alcoholism.")

If it's an *involuntary* disability, that means alcoholics don't choose to be alcoholics—it's not a case of "I'm going to grow up to be an alcoholic just like Mommy."

Also, the *characteristics* of the *disease* are defined by the *characteristics* of *those who have it*—the best way of figuring out what alcoholism is would be to go to an A.A. meeting (or other meeting of alcoholics) and look around at the characteristics of those who have it.

Also, since it's a *disease*, those who have it are worse off than those who don't.

The *involuntary* doesn't mean that alcoholics don't make a choice to drink (I believe they do, pretty much), but it *does* mean they don't make a choice to be alcoholics. But no fair saying, "I'm an alcoholic, so what I do is drink. It's only my nature." I'm sorry—that doesn't cut it. We *can* embrace what we *must* embrace: we can be sober, even though we're alco-holics. We can change our behavior; we can change our minds; we can change our brains.

A "disease condition" seems to be what is sometimes called a *predisposi-tion*, and that's the word I'd like to use here. A *predisposition* means there's something about the body that makes it likely a certain disease (or other event) will occur. In other words (in the alcoholism case), there could be a tendency in my body—my physical make-up—toward developing the "disease" of alcoholism. There seems to be evidence that this tendency could be inherited.

I should say here that in my early days, a more experienced A.A. named Jane R. told me alcoholism was a spiritual, mental, and physical disease. That wasn't original with her—it's in the literature—but what I took from that was not any particular definition of *disease*, but the emphasis on the *mental*, *physical*, and *spiritual*—the threefold distinction between the illness of *mind*, of *body*, and of *spirit*. I didn't care if it was illness, sickness, or disease. I did and do care that it is mental, physical, and spiritual.

How do I know if I have "alcoholism"?

How do I know if I have "alcoholism"? Elvin Morton Jellinek, then of Yale (who developed the Jellinek Curve and Jellinek types of alcoholism), suggested some answers to that a long long time ago, and while they've fallen out of favor, no one has found a good way to replace them. Here is the "down-sloping" side of the famous Jellinek Curve. (The "up-sloping" side is the "recovery" or "sobriety" side.) I've divided the twenty-eight stages into four sections of seven each, describing the progress of the disease, at least for Jellinek types alpha, beta, gamma, and delta. (The epsilon alcoholic doesn't seem to progress in the same way.) The idea of the Jellinek Curve is that if any part of this progress seems to describe what is happening to *you*, that gives a diagnosis and prognosis of your disease.

THE JELLINEK CURVE

The first seven

(1) Occasional relief drinking.
(2) Constant relief drinking starts.
(3) Increase in alcohol tolerance.
(4) Stuporous drinking.
(5) Onset of memory loss while drinking (blackouts).
(6) Increase in alcohol dependence.
(7) Urgency of the first drink.

The second seven

(8) Feelings of guilt.
(9) Unable to discuss problem (denial).
(10) Blackouts increase.
(11) Cannot stop when others do.
(12) Excuses made for drinking.
(13) Grandiose and aggressive behavior.
(14) Persistent remorse.

The next seven

(15) Loss of other interests.
(16) Geographic changes made.
(17) Avoiding family and friends.
(18) Work problems.
(19) Financial difficulty.
(20) Neglect of food.
(21) Early morning drinks.

The final seven

(22) Drinking with "inferiors" (radical change in friends).
(23) Moral deterioration.
(24) Loss of alcoholic tolerance.
(25) Physical complications.
(26) Onset of lengthy intoxication.
(27) Brain damage.
(28) Incarceration [jails or institutions] or death.

That's the progress Jellinek analyzed back in the 1940s and 1950s, using testimony from members of Alcoholics Anonymous. The "Curve" is still widely used, though not always in this country.

There's another question or set of questions we can ask: What does alcoholism do for me? What does alcohol do for me it doesn't do for non-alcoholics? The whole point is that, if you're an alcoholic, that means you react differently to alcohol from the way non-alcoholics react—and because of your body chemistry, alcohol will also interact differently with you. (As an example, alcohol can stimulate neurotransmission in alcoholics but slow it down in non-alcoholics.)

These differences were the point of the "controlled drinking" that was suggested to me in 1969 as a test of whether I was an alcoholic—I was told, and my experience has supported this, that alcoholics pretty much can't control their drinking *over the longer run*—even though we may be able to control it for a couple of days when we're trying to prove we're not alcoholics.

What *is* the longer run where we can't control our drinking? For me, it was only a few minutes before I was out of control, the very night I began the experiment. Others can control it for months or even (rarely) years. There are other tests, some of them better than others. The test suggested by the AMA definitions is simply to go to an A.A. meeting, look around, and see if you can identify with the people there.

My own experience is that it is very hard to identify with "the people there" when you first come in. But if you are an alcoholic, then as time goes on, you will hear stories that resemble your own. The saying goes "Some are sicker than others." I was one of the sicker ones. It took me a half-dozen meetings, "controlled drinking" that rapidly became uncontrolled, and a year of further decline (as measured on the Jellinek Chart), before I could admit I was an alcoholic. Many don't take this long—and some take even longer. Furthermore, I believe the old adage, that no one gets to A.A. by mistake, so if I'm hanging out at these meetings wanting to know if I qualify, the chances are pretty strong that just by the fact I'm there I qualify—people who don't have a problem with alcohol don't worry about having a problem with alcohol (and if the people close to you think you have a problem you can bet your sweet bippy you do).

You see, all alcoholics seem to have in common what the doctors call an idiopathic or idiosyncratic (or even "group idiopathic" or "group idiosyncratic") reaction to alcohol—meaning alcoholics react differently from other people. I am told it may have something to do with dopamine levels (which may be low in alcoholics), with acetylcholine/norepinephrine levels (I'm not sure whether these are low or high or simply easily altered). I am told it may have something to do with the effects on or of endorphins.

Dopamine, acetylcholine, norepinephrine—these are all involved with "neurotransmission," which is the way signals get from one place to another in the body and brain, where they go, how strong they are, what they signal, how easily they are received. Endorphins fall in the same category. The point is, alcoholics have a different ("idiopathic" or "idiosyncratic") brain and body chemistry from other people, so they react differently from other people—but like each other!

What do I do now?

What I just said is part of the good news—if you are an alcoholic, you can identify with other alcoholics. The rest of the good news is, you can change your patterns of neurotransmission. Yes, you were born with them, and at some point along the way (or maybe instantaneously with the first drink), they became what scientists call "potentiated"—that is, they changed from being *potential* (an inherited *tendency* or *predisposition*), to being *actual.* Nevertheless, though actual, they can now be changed again. How do you go about this second change? There seems to be general agreement around the world that the Twelve Steps invented by Alcoholics Anonymous in the 1930s are "The Way" or at least steps on The Way—but before we get to them, I want to do a little stage-setting, having to do with thinking patterns and perception.

In this stage-setting, we have begun the process of sobriety—and after a period of sobriety, our alcoholic thinking begins to go down the tubes. First of all, abstinence takes over. That is, when there is no alcohol in the brain, no alcohol in the central nervous system, no alcohol affecting the neurotransmitters, we become "natural" once again. We add to this the Twelve Steps and all that they require of us—relationship with a Higher Power, helping other alcoholics, eating on a regular basis, and even sleeping on a regular basis—sometimes for the first time in years we are actually sleeping rather than passing out!

For me sobriety was a step out into the sunshine and we all know what sunshine does for our mind and body. I also resumed my swimming—boy was that good for me! We put all of this together—relationship with a

Higher Power, helping others, eating, sleeping, functioning "normally" and not drinking—and we have gone from active alcoholic to sober alcoholic. We're still alcoholics but not much of anything else about us is the same as when we drank. We've all seen the bumper sticker "If it works don't fix it" and we have something here (A.A.) that really works.

There's an argument I've heard in A.A. about whether we're *recovered* alcoholics or *recovering* alcoholics. Officially (in my understanding) we're *recovered*—we aren't active alcoholics any more. But if we want to remind ourselves that the alcoholism may still be there, lurking—just as a cancer patient may have triumphed over one or another outbreak, or the tuberculosis patient may have seen this or that particular spot come off the lung, but the cancer may come again or the spot on the lungs—then, if that way of looking at things works for you, don't fix it! If you can stay sober more easily if you say *recovered*, say *recovered*. If you can stay sober more easily if you say *recovering*, say *recovering*. If you don't know, say what your sponsor thinks is best. If your sponsor has no opinion (highly unlikely in my book), flip a coin.

That reminds me of a friend of mine in the area where I live now. "If you don't know what to do [strictly speaking, which of two alternatives to pick], flip a coin!" If it's an important decision you will be guided (or told by your sponsor) what to do. If it's not, then don't waste time on it. *First things first!*—and this isn't a first thing, or you would have been guided or told, if you really wanted to know, and possibly even if you didn't.

Where does alcoholism come from?

Some of the answers to "What is alcoholism?" include or imply answers to this question, particularly the answers that talk about family inheritance. Fifty years ago, Elvin Jellinek, working with the Yale Laboratory of Applied Physiology and the Yale Summer School of Alcohol Studies, set out his classification of alcoholics. He called them alpha-alcoholics, beta-alcoholics, gamma-alcoholics, delta-alcoholics, and epsilon-alcoholics, each having some different sets of characteristics. "Alpha" alcoholism is a purely psychological continual reliance upon the effect of alcohol to relieve bodily or emotional pain. It is not progressive and has no withdrawal symptoms. "Beta" alcoholism is alcohol consumption leading to alcohol-related medical disorders, with neither physical nor psychological dependence, and no withdrawal symptoms.

"Gamma" alcoholism leads to "(1) acquired increased tissue tolerance to alcohol, (2) adaptive cell mechanism, (3) withdrawal symptoms and 'craving,' i.e., physical dependence, and (4) loss of control." This is the progressive fatal disease we usually think of as alcoholism—our *Alcoholism-1*—and it's the alcoholism of the Jellinek curve.

"Delta" alcoholism is pretty much the same as "gamma" alcoholism, but with inability to abstain in place of loss of control as the fourth symptom: it is also progressive. "Epsilon" alcoholism involves periodic bouts of drinking which can cause serious damage—sometimes called binge drinking. There has been a lot of recent attention paid to the "binge" version of "epsilon" alcoholism and what it includes. There has been argument about Jellinek's classifications and all classifications—but they suggest that those who have looked at the evidence do find different kinds of alcoholics, with different progressions of the "disease."

Saying this disease is "multigenic" would mean there isn't just one gene that carries this inheritance—but also that it *is* an inheritance. One clue as to whether I'm an alcoholic is whether I come from an alcoholic family. In my case, there's some evidence that "alcoholism"—the *predisposition*—existed in both my mother's family *and* my father's family. In my mother's family there was certainly alcoholism *and* a lot of heavy drinking. My mother stopped drinking at fifty-five—she had been widowed at thirty-five and became a full-blown alcoholic in less then six months; she was sober thirteen years when she died. My mother's father turned to solitary drinking after my grandmother died in her middle forties, leaving six children.

In my father's family, there are some "possible alcoholics"—including a heavy-drinking great uncle I never knew—but there's no question which side of my family had the stronger alcoholic tendency. The only family member with my heritage on both sides was my brother, and he had no doubt he was an alcoholic. He was a periodic. He stopped drinking two years after I did (he was twenty-eight, came to A.A., and died twenty-three years sober at the early age of fifty-one).

Now, since I have this "disease" (and my mother and my brother had it), I've wondered a lot about where it came from—o.k., probably it's hereditary, but why did it start out? I know my reflections on this aren't evidence, but most human diseases, like everything else humans inherit, originally had something useful about them. There must have been a reason for people to develop a special sensitivity/insensitivity to alcohol. It must, as the geneticists say, have had some survival value. Why would there be alcoholic families? Are there alcoholic families?

Are there alcoholic families?

Here we begin to go beyond and around and inside the surface evidence to make some suggestions, based on what we know about the way things work generally. If our body's biochemistry developed partly in response to outside conditions (as the textbooks tell us) and comes from a time when that biochemistry "conferred a survival value," then the various kinds of alcoholism must have had benefits back in time somewhere in the evolutionary process. By understanding how things got the way they are, we can perhaps see how they might be changed. A brief look at history tells me a special usefulness for alcohol sensitivity may have come thousands of years ago when bards were singing their songs, chanting their lays, warriors were roaming the land and feasting at night, and spirits like wine and mead at least spurred them on their way—and may have done more.

The special responses to alcohol, recalling these times, came to us through the ages, and here we are, still writing poetry and carrying on our battles, and drinking and feasting. Some believe that these spirits played a role in inventing human speech. I don't know how much of this is true history, but I know I have read it and have friends that have read it, and the tendency to use these substances has been with us from the beginning of our humanity. And, you know, if the parts of the brain that have to do with alcoholism also have to do with speech (and they seem to), then it's possible certain kinds of speech might combat our alcoholism, perhaps because "alcoholism" and linguistic abilities have something to do with each other. Maybe the leap into human speech had something to do with humans drinking, and maybe the development of alcoholism-2 (the *predisposition*)—of alcoholics' special reactions to alcohol—had something to do with the need for inspired speech at intervals.

If there's a premium on getting the "good" effects of alcohol more efficiently—which alcoholics do—then the families who need these effects more efficiently will be likely to be families of alcoholics. In Celtic cultures, for example, both druids and bards drank the sacred mead (fermented honey) for their ordained purposes. In Greek cultures, oracles and sibyls drank wine—as did devotees of the gods Bacchus and Dionysius. The wine or the mead was—but only for some—the gateway to the gods and to inspired speech. And who was part of the *some* was set by heredity—it ran in families. But in our times, in our society, alcohol no longer has that advantage—except perhaps for some creative writers. And it has lots of disadvantages—like jails, institutions, and (untimely) death.

CHAPTER II

What Is Sobriety?

Is sobriety the same thing as not drinking? We need to begin by asking, *What is the first qualification of sobriety?* For me, the first qualification of sobriety is that my system is free of alcohol and other destructive mind-altering substances. That's the beginning, and it's necessary. But simply not drinking or not "using" isn't the only thing. The idea is that we are to be sober not only in body, but also in mind and soul (or spirit). Only in this way can we be truly in touch with our higher power and our fellow man. My definition of sobriety has to do with living totally sober.

But this begins with not drinking wine, beer, whiskey, vodka, or any other form of alcohol—not using illegal "recreational" drugs, even marijuana—not developing a "sleeping pill" habit or becoming dependent on the use of mood-elevators to produce an artificial euphoria. At the beginning of Chapter I, I talked about the way I used tranquilizers for years—mostly Valium—while I was still drinking. In order to obtain real sobriety I not only had to quit drinking Dewar's White Label Blended Scotch Whisky, I also had to stop taking those tranquilizers—those little pills were destroying my life just as much as the alcohol was.

When I got sober, the A.A. old timers would not sponsor you at all if you were taking tranquilizers, sleeping pills, or what they called mood-elevators. They were opposed to anything which goes to our central nervous system and affects our ability to think clearly—their idea was that if we're taking something that muddles our thinking, then our thinking isn't what it would be. There was an important warning there.

This can be a complicated and difficult issue. My brother died twenty-three years sober at the age of fifty-one, in great pain. The fact that he took pain-relieving medication on doctor's orders doesn't mean that he didn't die sober—he did. But killing the pain was part of his dying, not his living sober. I do not know when and in what amounts it is proper for an alcoholic living sober to take painkillers (beyond aspirin and the like). I do know that I have had problems, as a sponsor, working with people taking major painkillers. It was hard to get through the drugs to the person.

As you will see in Chapter VI, I am not only alcoholic but also manic-depressive (bi-polar), which means partly that my system lacks a natural balance, one that can be more or less restored by taking lithium carbonate. So for thirty-four years now I have taken daily doses of lithium carbonate, an unpleasant rather than a pleasant experience. I myself do not—for various medical reasons—take either first- or second-generation antidepressants. No direct experience there. But I can say that I have had problems, as a sponsor, working with people taking antidepressants of any generation. It was hard to get through the drugs to the person.

What comes after getting rid of the alcohol (and other substances)? Once that freedom from alcohol and other harmful substances is accomplished, sobriety is a mindset learned from regular attendance at meetings, from practicing the Twelve Steps, from a close relationship with a sponsor, from regular prayer and meditation, and from "giving it away." As I said before, for me, sobriety was a step out into the sunshine. We put together our relationship with a Higher Power, helping others, eating right, sleeping, functioning "normally" and not drinking—and we have gone from active alcoholic to sober alcoholic. We're still alcoholics but not much of anything else about us is the same as when we drank. We can—and frequently do—act the same way we acted when we were drinking (except that we're not drinking). Some people call this state of being a "dry drunk."

Let's also talk a little bit about some other points that have to do with living a sober life. Remember the questions as we asked them in the Introduction—*Why meetings? What do you mean by "practicing" the Twelve Steps?* (there's more on this second question in Chapter III)—*What's this about a sponsor? About prayer and meditation? About "giving it away"?*—you see, these are all, by my experience, part of living a sober life. And one more question about getting completely sober, *What about emotional sobriety?*

Why attend meetings?

The interesting thing about attending meetings is that just about any alcoholic I have ever known has *never* attended meetings "just for the hell of it"—I always had a sponsor going to meetings I went to (or I went to the meetings she went to), and my friends were also there going to meetings I went to—originally probably to see that I went. For some reason most alcoholics have a tendency to be loners before they get sober and when we try to stop drinking and live the better life we find we can't do it as a loner; we find we have to be *part of*—part of the other people, of the places and activities that bring us all together as a unit, discarding the life of the solitary drinker.

Meetings are informative (if we listen), meetings are friendly (if we are willing), and I have heard it said that every A.A. meeting raises the level of consciousness of every alcoholic there. When I look at the level of my consciousness when I got sober, I see I was in a world of alcoholic paranoia, a world of thinking of myself, a world without a relationship with a Higher Power, a world that wasn't close to my fellow man. My life since then tells me that my level of consciousness has been raised: I am no longer any of those things (mostly not, anyway).

My thinking now (mostly) runs along the lines of asking, how can I help the other person? I have an instinct (but it's a *learned* instinct and it's part of my sober life)—an instinct for love for people I know and people I don't know—and my goal is to stay sober and to carry the message to the alcoholic who still suffers. Those who don't understand why A.A. works or how it works or does it work or can it work might want to spend some time going around to these meetings and their questions might be answered. Or not, because we can often resist answers. There's a line often quoted in A.A., ostensibly from Herbert Spencer but it actually seems to be based on something the eighteenth-century philosopher William Paley once said, about "contempt prior to investigation" being a recipe for failure. I've known it to happen.

What are the Twelve Steps?

These are the Twelve Steps: (1) We admitted we were powerless over alcohol—that our lives had become unmanageable, (2) Came to believe that a Power greater than ourselves could restore us to sanity, (3) Made a decision to turn our will and our lives over to the care of God *as we understood Him*, (4) Made a searching and fearless moral inventory of ourselves, (5) Admitted to God, to ourselves, and to another human being the exact nature of our wrongs, (6) Were entirely ready to have God remove all these defects of character, (7) Humbly asked Him to remove our shortcomings, (8) Made a list of all persons we had harmed, and became willing to make amends to them all, (9) Made direct amends to such people wherever possible, except when to do so would injure them or others, (10) Continued to take personal inventory and when we were wrong, promptly admitted it, (11) Sought through prayer and meditation to improve our conscious contact with God *as we understood Him*, praying only for knowledge of His will for us and the power to carry that out, and (12) Having had a spiritual awakening as the result of these steps, we tried to carry this message to alcoholics, and to practice these principles in all our affairs. [Reprinted with permission]

These have a chapter all to themselves. But right here let me say the word "practice" at the very end of the steps is one of the things that is important, and if "practice doesn't make perfect" here, at least it gets us along the road.

What is a sponsor?

When I asked Kay H. to be my sponsor (one of the smartest moves I ever made) she told me what would be expected of me: don't drink—go to meetings—call your sponsor—read the Big Book—go to a Step Meeting every week—and in those days before disposable styrofoam containers I washed coffee cups in the kitchen every week. *My sponsor told me what to do to be sober and stay sober, and my sponsor was my model for a sober life.* And your sponsor should have a sponsor, so you can have a grand-sponsor. Which brings us to the next question—*what is a sponsor?*

Essentially, a sponsor was and is an "experienced" sober A.A. who could guide the newcomer into the program. At the beginning, of course, Alcoholics Anonymous functioned as a kind of secret fellowship, and one had to be sponsored to be present at the meeting. Sponsorship seems originally to have been a one-on-one relationship established to get the newcomer through the Steps (at least the first time) and fully into the fellowship. We believe it may have begun formally in Cleveland A.A. with a man named Clarence. Dr. Bob, with his huge vocabulary of outdated slang, his ready laughter, and his gentle self-mockery, called those he sponsored his *pigeons*—like homing pigeons, they came home to roost; like any pigeons they made a lot of noise and not a little mess, *and never had any money.* They have been called *babies* (which preserves something of the original idea of sponsorship), and they are now frequently called *sponsees,* which is a kind of short-hand for "the person I sponsor (in Alcoholics Anonymous)."

What about prayer and meditation?

Prayer and meditation are elaborated on in our Eleventh Step— "Sought through prayer and meditation to improve our conscious contact with God *as we understood Him,* praying only for knowledge of His will for us and the power to carry that out." You will notice on the wording that there is no definite or specific religious theory presented. This step, like all of Alcoholics Anonymous, leaves the interpretation of God or the Higher Power up to the members. When I came to A.A, I had no interpretation of God—I had a rough experience as a small child and I was very skeptical of "this God stuff." I was told to put my fears aside and pray anyway. I was told that was part of a sober life.

I did that—I prayed—and it was helpful to me to think there was indeed a power greater than I was, who was here to help me. Meditation, on the other hand, which is often difficult for many, was no less so for me. I had been a heavy alcohol user, had a lot of electric shock treatments, and had used a lot of tranquilizers. I thought my mind was blown. I truly believed I could never meditate. I got a book on meditation and I got meditation tapes, but I was not successful until I met another sponsor, Big Book Mary of Willow Grove, Pennsylvania.

Mary told me we can all meditate—these Twelve Steps are for all of us—and I was no exception. (This story is told more fully in Chapter V.) So I went to Mary's house after work every afternoon. We read a passage for meditation. Mary began to meditate. I sat there, silent. Her mind became very quiet—and eventually the same thing happened to me. I have taught many people to meditate the way Mary taught me and have had groups in my home where everyone in the group learned to meditate. The key, to me, is doing it with someone who has experience—who has the "skill." The benefit of meditation is that it helps clear our thinking and helps ease the channels to and from God as we understand Him and it quells the racing mind. I've never known anyone who has not directly benefited from mastering this skill and I believe—with Mary—that probably all alcoholics have this gift. But like any other gift, it requires practice to make full—or even good—use of it.

What about "giving it away"?

Giving it away is elaborated on in A.A.'s Step Twelve—"Having had a spiritual awakening as the result of these steps, we tried to carry this message to alcoholics, and to practice these principles in all our affairs." It should be very evident that in order to have anything to help anyone else we must have spent time going through the program—through the process of sobriety—and after we have had a spiritual awakening (usually defined as being different inside from what we were before), we carry this message of the way to sobriety by speaking at meetings, by sharing at meetings, by going on a call when someone asks for help, by picking someone up and bringing them to a meeting, setting up a meeting—all involving experience, knowledge, and a desire to help.

Two big factors in giving it away are (1) that "you have to give it away to keep it" and (2) that "you have to have it to give it away." Both are part of giving it away—and both are part of sobriety. Remember, one of the things sobriety is, is a process. In that process, we learn how to be sober—not just to "stay sober" in the sense of not picking up a drink, but to live a sober life, emotionally sober, spiritually sober, mentally sober. I'll come back to the matter of being emotionally sober, but being sober in all these ways gives us something we need ("you have to have it to give it away") and then we keep that something by imparting it to other people ("you have to give it away to keep it"). There's a reading in one of the meditation books widely used by A.A.s (the *Twenty-Four Hour* book) that makes this a little clearer to me—it's the entry for November 2nd, part of which is quoted as an epigraph for this book: "Keep yourself like an empty vessel for God to fill. Keep pouring yourself out to help others so that God can keep filling you up with His spirit. The more you give, the more you will have for yourself." This business of "keeping it by giving it away" isn't a paradox—it's a clear rule for keeping yourself open for something to come in.

What is that *something*? The meditation book talks about God's spirit. However you want to express it, I think that, fundamentally, it's our experience in staying sober, our spiritual strength gained by being sober, and our hope from seeing the process of sobriety in ourselves and in others. That's customarily abbreviated as "sharing our experience, strength, and hope"—but it's not the experience of *drinking* (all alcoholics have that)—it's the experience of *sobriety* that is important here. And part of that's the mindset we talked about at the beginning of this section.

I said I'd write a little more about this matter of emotional sobriety. The problem is, even after we've stopped drinking—and maybe after we've stopped drinking for quite a while—we still are liable to go on emotional binges that lead to what have been called emotional hangovers. We say things we wish we hadn't said. We "lose it." We really feel physically sick—and certainly sick at heart—the next day. There's a list of qualities we need to do the Ninth Step (listed in the *12 & 12*)—good judgment, a careful sense of timing, courage, and prudence: those are the qualities of a sober life. In old times, people called the first two justice and temperance, and all four together were called the cardinal virtues. These four virtues (justice, temperance, courage, and prudence) were the key to living a righteous life.

What about emotional sobriety?

Let me give some examples of emotional sobriety (or its opposite) in my experience of the struggle to live (as the old prayer says) "a godly, righteous, and sober life." (That's from a prayer Bill W. heard every night at the Calvary Mission when he was first getting sober.) I have heard many times at meetings of sober alcoholics (men and women, though more frequently men) who confess to road rage when other drivers act the way other drivers do—cutting them off, tailgating them, driving ten miles under the speed limit in no passing areas in clear weather, and so on. Some of these are alcoholics who have been sober quite a number of years. But road rage is not a characteristic of sobriety. Suppose I'm at a meeting where you share without being called on—spontaneously—and I try three or four times to speak and get cut off every time. Now I can say to myself, I'm not supposed to be sharing tonight, I'm supposed to be listening, and listen carefully to what the others are saying. But even if I do this, I have to watch out for the devil on my shoulder that tells me what they're saying isn't as good or useful or understanding as what I would have said. That's not road rage, and it's better than my getting angry at the meeting (certainly better than my walking out), but it's not emotional sobriety either. I have to watch out also for statements or catch-phrases (at meetings or elsewhere) that set me off—emotional triggers, some would call them.

In short, I'm supposed to be emotionally sober, to act like the mature responsible adult I never really was before I came into A.A. I have to give up all those lines like "Don't get angry, get even!" and not even substitute lines like "This too shall pass!" or "I accept it but I don't have to like it!" Resignation and pretend "acceptance" (which is really just sitting there all sullen and sulky and surly, and isn't really acceptance) are not part of the sober life. For me, they're part of something in between sobriety and a "dry drunk"—maybe closer to sobriety but not there yet. It's like the passage in Second Corinthians also used as an epigraph for this book—"Give not grudgingly, or of necessity, for God loveth a cheerful giver." When we get truly sober, we don't do what we have to do because we have to do it, we do it joyfully (that's part of what humility means) out of our own will, because we want to. "How long do I have to go to meetings?" the newcomer asked. "Until you want to," the sponsor answered. That's the matter in a nutshell.

Let me quote Bill W. on emotional sobriety—it's well worth quoting and reading (from the *12 & 12*, pp. 88-89, in the chapter on Step Ten): "When a drunk has a terrific hangover because he drank heavily yesterday, he can't live well today. But there is another kind of hangover which we all experience whether we are drinking or not. That is the emotional hangover, the direct result of yesterday's and sometimes today's excesses of negative emotion—anger, fear, jealousy, and the like. If we would live serenely today and tomorrow, we certainly need to eliminate these hangovers. This doesn't mean we need to wander morbidly around in the past. It requires an admission and correction of errors *now*. Our inventory enables us to settle with the past. When this is done we are ready to leave it behind us. When our inventory is carefully taken, and we have made peace with ourselves, the conviction follows that tomorrow's challenges can be met as they come."

This is Bill W. (I think) at his most characteristic. He diagnoses a condition we all recognize, emotional binge followed by emotional hangover, then sorts it out and notes the corrective measures to be followed. And in doing this, he emphasizes that the Steps (in this particular case the Tenth Step) are the key to living the sober life, as my sponsor Kay H. long ago pointed out. In Chapter IV we look at some of the slogans widely heard in A.A., and we'll see that they too can help guide us in the way of a sober life.

And one thing more. There's a disagreement in A.A. over whether there's a difference between "dry" and "sober" or whether it's all sobriety, and the only question is the quality of the sobriety. Unfortunately (in my view) the phrase "quality of sobriety" is sometimes used as a weapon against "quantity of sobriety"—saying in effect, it doesn't matter how long you're sober, it's the quality of your sobriety that counts. That's true, of course, but it's been my own experience over the years, looking at others who have been sober longer than I, that greater length of sobriety indicates a wider variety of problems successfully faced, of questions successfully answered, and of temptations overcome—so frequently quality and quantity can go together. Be that as it may, the difference between saying "sober *vs.* dry" on the one hand and saying "good sobriety *vs.* not-so-good sobriety" on the other is so much a semantic difference and so little a difference in defining a goal, that it falls in the "flip a coin" category. The important point is, there is a sober lifestyle, a sober mindset, and while they begin with not taking a drink, that's not where they end. It used to be said (perhaps it still is in some areas) that the first "commandment" of A.A. was "Don't drink and go to meetings!"—but the great "commandment" was "Trust in God and clean house!" Sobriety as I understand it requires both.

CHAPTER III

What Are the Twelve Steps?

Here are the Twelve Steps as set up in the A.A. Big Book—*Alcoholics Anonymous,* all four editions (1939, 1955, 1976, 2001). These steps are also given and elaborated on in a second book, called the *Twelve Steps and Twelve Traditions* (the *12 & 12*), which was also written by Bill W.

1) We admitted we were powerless over alcohol—that our lives had become unmanageable.

2) Came to believe that a Power greater than ourselves could restore us to sanity.

3) Made a decision to turn our will and our lives over to the care of God *as we understood Him.*

4) Made a searching and fearless moral inventory of ourselves.

5) Admitted to God, to ourselves, and to another human being the exact nature of our wrongs.

6) Were entirely ready to have God remove all these defects of character.

7) Humbly asked Him to remove our shortcomings.

8) Made a list of all persons we had harmed, and became willing to make amends to them all.

9) Made direct amends to such people wherever possible, except when to do so would injure them or others.

10) Continued to take personal inventory and when we were wrong, promptly admitted it.

11) Sought through prayer and meditation to improve our conscious contact with God *as we understood Him*, praying only for knowledge of His will for us and the power to carry that out.

12) Having had a spiritual awakening as the result of these steps, we tried to carry this message to alcoholics, and to practice these principles in all our affairs.

[Reprinted by permission]

So this is a list of the steps, from one to twelve, but we still have to ask the question, *What Are the Twelve Steps?* What I'm going to talk about here is what they have meant to me.

What Is the First Step?

The First Step is, **We admitted we were powerless over alcohol—that our lives had become unmanageable.** In very early sobriety the easiest way for me to remember the First Step and the implications of powerlessness and unmanageability—the two go together—was by remembering my last drink, which was the most powerless and unmanageable time of my life. There's the old saying in A.A., "If you can't remember your last drink, perhaps you haven't had it!"—I've made an effort to remember my last drink and as long as that's at the forefront of my mind the evidence of powerlessness and unmanageability is there. When I tell my story I remind myself of what happened to me when I couldn't get any more alcohol that last night—there was no more alcohol in my house—and I was completely out of control.

Before that night I always thought I was in control of my drinking (my experiment with "controlled drinking" the year before should have made me realize I wasn't)—I believed I could "stop and start at any time"—but the last night that I drank was definite proof to me that I was out of control, that I was powerless over alcohol—that alcohol had taken over my life. Alcohol had the power—I didn't. As to the unmanageability—I became out of control and I blamed the person responsible for the fact there was no alcohol in the house for the way I felt—and I blamed him for my ensuing behavior. I attempted bodily harm that night and I believe I had murder in my heart, all because I had no alcohol—not because anyone had tried to harm me but because I had no alcohol. At the root was the fact

I wasn't managing things at all—I couldn't manage things at all. My anger was my last resistance to accepting this.

It's my very strong hope that I never forget my last drink and all that it's meant to me and all that it means to me. For me, the powerlessness and the unmanageability were both part of the same thing—for me it's not two separate but two linked characteristics. It's often said in A.A. that the First Step is the only one that "we have to work perfectly every day." It's sometimes even said that the First Step has not two but *three* main parts—not only *powerlessness* over alcohol and *unmanageability* of life, but also the key word *admission*. The admission is the thing that must be done, that must be worked perfectly every day. It's sometimes said—and I believe it—that there are *four* parts, *four* key words, beginning with the very first word, *We.* When I tell my story at a meeting—when I share at a meeting—when I remember that last night openly at a meeting—that's part of the *We.* That's part of "How It Works."

What Is the Second Step?

The Second Step is, ***Came to believe that a Power greater than ourselves could restore us to sanity.*** What I think about this Second Step is hard for me to put into words, but let's begin by saying that, for me, as long as I'm not drunk and not in a straitjacket, I'm in the process of being restored to sanity. In the *12 & 12* Bill defines "sanity" as "soundness of mind"—we're not talking technical definitions here, but ordinary speech. (In any case, "insane" is a legal term not a psychiatric one, and alcoholics are not legally insane—they do know the difference between right and wrong!) In fact I haven't been able to find the word "insanity" used in A.A. literature, though I've often heard a definition of "alcoholic insanity" as continuing to do the same thing [drink] and expecting different results. In other words, alcoholic thinking is somewhat out of kilter, but not psychotic.

The really hard part of Step Two for me was the part about a Higher Power. Many of us have difficulties about the "Higher Power," God, and I'm no exception. I had to overcome that. My difficulties in this area began in my childhood when my father died when I was twelve. After growing up

in Sunday School, church, church suppers, church musicales, my brother
and I were told we would have no more church, no more Sunday School,
because of what God did to our Daddy. Of course at the time I had no idea
what an impact this would have in every corner of my life—that's the kind
of thing you learn when you have told your story many times over the years.
This period marked the time when an awful lot of difficulty began for me:
leaving school to work in my family's business—my Daddy's greenhouses—
at thirteen, my first drink at fourteen, my first suicide attempt at fifteen, my
first psychiatrist at sixteen. I never saw the connection between the events
of my life and my lack of any spiritual activity. By the time I got to
Alcoholics Anonymous, I couldn't pray, wouldn't pray, and didn't see the
reason to pray. And I've heard so many others with the same thinking—
how can a "Higher Power" have anything to do with *my sanity*?

I guess there are a lot of ways to approach this. Some take the gamble
and begin to pray here and there (for starters); some just take it for granted
they'll be restored; some take it for granted they won't be restored (they
have trouble). Some, like me, follow orders ("suggestions") and pray even
though they don't believe. I did that and then I came to the very quick
conclusion, since *I wasn't in a straitjacket, I wasn't in a hospital, I hadn't had
a drink*—I must be on the road to sanity. It worked.

What Is the Third Step?

The Third Step is, ***Made a decision to turn our will and our lives over to
the care of God* as we understood Him.** Making a decision about anything—should I take a bath or a shower?—should I vacuum today or
tomorrow?—should I have lunch now or later?—making a decision of any
kind at all is frequently tough even for the best of us. But this is a place—
this Third Step place—where we must make the decision. No one else can
make it for us. And it has to be a real decision—no putting on funny hats
and playing children's games, no holding back, no maybe, no "on the one
hand—on the other hand."

And then there's the problem of turning our lives and our will over to
anything or anyone. We tell ourselves that we don't have to do this,

because "we know we can take care of these things ourselves"—I'm sorry, but experience proves to the contrary. The only part I play is turning it over to his care, relying on my Higher Power as a young child relies on the parent. And then, we're supposed to be turning our lives and our will over to the care of "God *as we understand Him*"? I'll tell you, I used to tell my sponsor, "But I don't understand Him"—as though that relieved me from Step Three. Who understands God (I asked)? When will I understand God? How will I understand God? I thought these were really big questions. But—and here's the point—"God as we understand Him" really means "as much of God as we understand today." Here's what Bill W.'s spiritual counselor told him when he was first getting sober: "The true meaning of faith is self-surrender to God.... Surrender to whatever you know about Him or believe must be the truth about Him. Surrender to Him, if necessary, in total ignorance of Him. Far more important that you touch Him than that you understand Him at first."

First of all, let's remember the operative word is *care*—just like we care for our children, care for our puppies or our kittens, it's the *care* of God for us that counts here. For me to keep it simple, I have to remember this—it's for me to make the decision to turn it over to the care of God, however much I understand of God—it's for Him to care. I still have to make all the daily decisions about what to do next—"What's the next thing I need to do today?"—but I need to remember every time I make one of these little daily decisions that there is a God who cares about what I decide, and who cares about what happens to me. I learned this about care when I was still having a lot of serious difficulty wanting to drink and my sponsor told me I had to develop a relationship with God or I would always want to drink. (Alcoholics have serious problems developing a relationship with anyone or anything.)

I told her my tale of woe and how I didn't believe. That's when she said you don't have to—pray anyway. That's when I began to learn about the care of God—I prayed that Serenity Prayer ten or twelve times a day and I have been so well cared for I still haven't had a drink. And that's just one example—every alcoholic has his or her own example about the care of God. I think that my not drinking is the care of God—it isn't something I do on my own by myself. There's a prayer Bill W. wrote to be said when the alcoholic takes the Third Step. "Many of us said to our Maker, *as we understood Him,* 'God, I offer myself to Thee—to build with me and do with me as Thou wilt. Relieve me of the bondage of self, that I may better do Thy will. Take away my difficulties, that victory over them may bear witness to those I would help of Thy power, Thy Love, and Thy Way of Life. May I do Thy will always!'" Remember that it says "God as *we* understood Him" and not "God as *I* understood Him." It's not me—it's all of us.

What Is the Fourth Step?

The Fourth Step is, *Made a searching and fearless moral inventory of ourselves.* An oldtimer where I got sober told me the key word is *moral*—I've heard others say the key word is *fearless.* Whichever it is, they're both important—maybe there's more than one key word. The moral inventory is not a listing of all of our crimes—every time we knocked over a gas station or held up a grocery store—it's not a criminal inventory but a moral inventory. That means I'm looking at my moral or immoral behavior, not my legal or illegal behavior.

When I did my Fourth Step, I looked at how honest I was with myself and with those I loved and with my employer. I found out that my grades on honesty with myself were fairly good, with my loved ones less good—I had a tendency to lie about myself to them, where I was going, what I was doing. With my employer and my business associates, my morals were even less satisfactory. I wasn't always prompt about when I came to work—that's robbing from my employer—and there was the time I spent out of my office visiting with my pals. And the numbers on my expense sheets were sometimes a work of fiction. I think these are the kinds of things included in a moral inventory.

And there's the "fearless" part. I had better get down to the nitty gritty—I had better look at all of my actions and transactions. Something else that's important here—it says it's an inventory *of ourselves.* I don't need to take anyone else's inventory no matter how much I may want to—there's no reason on God's green earth for me to take anyone's but my own.

For years I told myself I had to take the other guy's inventory so I would know how not to do it. Not so—and thank God I no longer feel this way. (That doesn't mean I'm perfect about not taking anyone else's inventory—but I'm a lot better.)

Some people do a Fourth-Step inventory on a regular basis—every year on their anniversary, for example. I have done it four or five times in thirty-five years. One of my very dearest friends in A.A. believed you only do this Fourth Step inventory one time. I think that's fine too—each person together with his or her sponsor makes the determination about when to do this Step. So long as we remember that it's a *moral* inventory and *fearless* and *thorough* and *of ourselves*, I don't think it matters how often we do it, *so long as we have done it.* Some people do it and recommend doing it with the Seven Deadly Sins (pride, anger, gluttony, greed, lust, envy, sloth) to help classify our actions. That was helpful to me when I did it that way—but I don't recommend it unless it fits in with the way you want to think.

One very important factor mentioned in the Big Book is the grudge list, where we list the grudges and gripes we have about others. The grudge list is on page 65 of the Big Book—it's recognizable because it's in an entirely different format from any other page in A.A. literature. I've done this grudge list several times and each time what it tells me is something (quite a lot) about myself, which is what I need. The Big Book mentions that in doing this, "we have written down a lot. We have listed and analyzed our resentments. We have begun to comprehend their futility and their fatality. We have commenced to see their terrible destructiveness." In fact, with luck, we have made what Bill calls a fair appraisal. What I had to watch out for, particularly, were difficulties from manic depression—the depression part that is pride in reverse, and the grandiose or self-righteous manic reaction that is pride pure and simple. But we'll talk a little more about that later.

What Is the Fifth Step?

The Fifth Step is, **Admitted to God, to ourselves, and to another human being the exact nature of our wrongs.** Many people are really terrified of

Step Five and I was among them. We just don't want anyone to know the deep dark secrets of our past, or especially the deep dark secrets of our hearts. I had vowed that I was never going to take Step Five—I had spent plenty of time in hospitals and with psychiatrists and with counselors and I never got better, so I really didn't see how a Fifth Step would help.

This Step is sometimes read (with emphasis on the words italicized here) as "Admitted to *God*, to ourselves, and to *another human being* the exact nature of our *wrongs*." But, after thirty-five years' experience, I think the proper reading is, "*Admitted* to God, to *ourselves*, and to *another human being* the *exact nature* of our wrongs." In the first case, what is important is that another human being is hearing a confession to God of wrongs done. That's the ancient practice of confession, there is nothing wrong with it, and it is indeed part of what Bill W. recommends. The second reading emphasizes the *admission* to *oneself*—as well as to God and another human being—of what one has done—in other words, part of the process of knowing oneself.

When I told my sponsor I wasn't going to do Step Five she was the essence of patience and tolerance—and decided she was going to wait me out. Before I got around to Step Five she died, and I had another hard time to get through. Meanwhile a very good friend of my sponsor took over and I did my Fifth Step one Saturday at her kitchen table: it was a very unusual experience for me. (When I tell my story I emphasize the fact that she knew where I was and stepped in to help me when Kay died.)

Her name was Mary K. and she started by telling me the purpose of Step Five and a few things from her own life—I was so surprised to hear these experiences coming from someone I had really looked up to—and I never would have thought she ever even crossed a street against the light. I was set up for this step—a perfect set-up—and I told her everything— things I was sure I would never tell anyone, I told Mary K. that day in her kitchen. I left her house that afternoon and when I was walking to my car I knew things were different. I wasn't the same—I was never going to be the same—and everything was all right. I didn't know what everything was, but I knew it was all right.

Here's what Bill says about Step Five. "We have a written inventory and we are prepared for a long talk.... We pocket our pride and go to it, illuminating every twist of character, every dark cranny of the past. Once we have taken this step, withholding nothing, we are delighted. We can look the world in the eye. We can be alone at perfect peace and ease. Our fears fall from us. We begin to feel the nearness of our creator. We may have had certain spiritual beliefs, but now we begin to have a spiritual experience.... We feel we are on the Broad Highway, walking hand in hand with the Spirit of the Universe." I think the reason this Fifth Step was so successful for me, when all the therapy sessions had failed, was that I was sitting across the table from a woman who was an alcoholic, and I could share myself with her and she was sharing herself with me.

That kind of thing had never happened to me before, though it has happened many times since—women have taken the Fifth Step with me at *my* kitchen table and I have taken mine several times again. This is one of those experiences that we never really hear about, never really know about, until one day it happens with us and we're changed forever. (The reason we don't know about it, can't hear about it, is that it has to happen to us before we can know, before we can even know what we're hearing.) I think that of all the steps this was the one that was truly pivotal in my sobriety—I was finally able to look at myself and say *O.K.*—which makes it much easier to work the rest of the steps, finally seeing ourselves on a more positive plane.

What Is the Sixth Step?

The Sixth Step is, *Were entirely ready to have God remove all these defects of character.* Step Six is the place where we take a break and review everything we've done so far in the first five steps. The idea is that we want to have everything in proper order and we want to be certain our work is solid before we go one bit further. Of course, Step Six is also preparation for Step Seven—and to me it is one of the clearer examples that all the Twelve Steps are a miracle.

You see, to me Step Six is not really a step in itself—it's a bridge. It's right there in the middle and leads us from Step Five to Steps Seven through

Twelve. We really can't go anywhere further along the road without it. Bill W. says this is the point at which we abandon limited objectives and move toward God's will for us. This is one of those places where we all remember what we were taught as kids—"Ready! Get set! Go!" We're entirely ready to get set and go to the rest of the steps—starting with Step Seven.

It says "*Became* entirely ready to have God remove all these defects of character," as though the conversion experience of the Fifth Step was necessary but might not be enough. Bill W. goes on—"It is plain for everybody to see that each sober A.A. member has been granted a release from this very obstinate and potentially fatal obsession [with alcohol]. So in a very complete and literal way, all A.A.s have 'become entirely ready' to have God remove the mania for alcohol from their lives" (*12 & 12* page 64). In short, willingness to clean house provides readiness for God's removal of the defects of character (flaws, sins, shortcomings). The linchpin is that "to be willing" is "to do"—the willingness is shown, if I may invent a word, in the doingness, in the constant doing that is Brother Lawrence's "practice of the presence of God"—a state of doing that is a spiritual state.

Step Six has grown from a checkpoint on the effects of a variety of religious experience in Step Five, to a spiritual exercise in its own right. In ordinary speech, there is a difference between *ready* and *willing*. I'm still thinking about the phrase "ready, willing, and able" or the old "ready—get set—go!" with its counterpart "on your mark—get set—go!" To be ready is to be on the mark, prepared, "with all our ducks in a row"—the gun loaded and "at the ready." Bill W. seems to be saying that complete willingness makes one ready—and the hole that will be left in our life if our sins and flaws are removed will itself be filled by God (and A.A.), if we are completely willing. But we must keep up the readiness, the preparedness. Eternal vigilance is the price of liberty.

Of course, except "the Lord build the house, they labor in vain that build it" (Psalm 127, first verse). But the house must be ready, swept clean, "redded up" for the new tenant. (That "redded up" is an Ulsterism that settled down and is still used where I live in Pennsylvania—I suppose it might have been "readied up" once.) Readiness includes willingness—in fact, readiness depends on willingness—and willingness without readiness is not true willingness. The two go together—but they aren't the same.

What Is the Seventh Step?

The Seventh Step is, *Humbly asked Him to remove our shortcomings.* The first word and the one most people think is most important is *humbly.* We have to come into this step with every bit of humility we can muster. We are humbly asking him for what is a really large order—which is removing our defects of character. Just speaking for myself, I believe I practiced this step in my early days with very little humility—I wasn't sure what humility was and I really didn't know if I had it—but I had some fearful defects of character and many years of therapy and counseling had failed to remedy one single defect of character—only God could remedy these as only God could remedy my desire to drink—so I asked pretty much out of desperation but without much humility—except that maybe the desperation was itself the beginning of humility.

With the experience of going to meetings, staying sober, being part of A.A., I've come to the conclusion that this is a terribly important step, and I've thought a lot before I used the word *terribly.* If we don't do it, the results are terrible, to us and to others. Now I can't get very far in the middle of a bout of anger or pride or lust—what kind of work can I do for the Father when I'm surrounded by my own difficulties? How many people can I sponsor with love and affection if I'm walking around in a state of anger or if I'm throwing books at people (one time I was so furious I threw two—yes, two!—prayer books—yes, prayer books!—at my husband. Thanks to this Step and all the others I haven't done that again to this day).

Once I've found out what these defects are (Step Four) and I've gone over them with God and another alcoholic (Step Five), then I've got to get about the business of cleaning up my side of the street. How much time can I spend in prayer and meditation—or how about doing a spot check inventory—if I'm walking around in gluttony? It just doesn't work. I have to have my side of the street clean before I go on. I have to. Bill tells us in the *12 & 12* that humility is the "avenue to true freedom of the human spirit"—an example of "strength from weakness"—that pain is the admission price to new life, self-centered fear is the chief activator of defects, and "Step Seven is a change in attitude which permits us to move out of ourselves toward God."

When we are in the proper state of mind and body and spirit—when we are ready to let God remove our defects—"we say something like this: 'My Creator, I am now willing that you should have all of me, good and bad. I pray that you now remove from me every single defect of character which stands in the way of my usefulness to you and my fellows. Grant me strength, as I go out from here, to do your bidding. Amen.' We have then completed *Step Seven*." (Big Book p. 76)

What Is the Eighth Step?

Step Eight is, **Made a list of all persons we had harmed, and became willing to make amends to them all.** This is much more than it appears at first glance. It is not just making a list of persons we had harmed. It is searching our backgrounds for the most complete list, the best possible list, that we can put together. I'm sure my background is not the only one smattered with people I wasn't really willing to make amends to—to search them out and bring my bad past behavior to the surface. And what about the people who treated me just as badly as I treated them? Perhaps I'm still harboring ill feelings. It was suggested to me I really pray for them.

There were two on my list I really had to pray for before I could really think about going to them. I used the procedure recommended in a story— "Freedom from Bondage"—in the back of the Big Book to get rid of resentment (p. 552 in the third and fourth editions). I had a lot of resentment in my mind to get rid of before I could be willing to make amends to every one on my list. As thorough as I thought I was in listing everyone on my Eighth Step list, a couple of years later a couple of other names came to the surface—so I wasn't as thorough as I thought I had been.

I started my list with the people closest to me, people I loved the most, people who had already forgiven me the most. I felt that I was demonstrating my sincerity not to live the way I had lived before, not to treat them the way I had treated them before. I don't think it was by design but it seemed that the people I loved less went toward the bottom of my list. There were some people who had already died. And there was one name on my list that my sponsor crossed off.

Over the years I think I assembled a pretty complete list—at least I certainly hope I have. I don't want to leave anyone out. I don't ever want to forget about anyone I failed to treat the way my parents taught me to treat people. Our literature doesn't say that this list is made up only of people who were in our lives during our drinking careers. It's made up of everybody we have harmed. When I think of the things I used to think were important in life—like being sarcastic and really putting someone down—I don't want to think for one minute that I would do those things again or that I would slight anyone by not having them on my list. Bad behavior is bad behavior—whenever it's done and whoever is the object. I don't want to walk around racing my mind over and over the things I did, but I don't want to slight or forget them either.

I know that alcoholics have been frequently told by their sponsor to keep their Fourth-Step lists. Why? Because they will be at the top of the Eighth-Step list. Pretty clearly, Step Eight builds on Steps Four and Five—after the alcoholic has gone through the spiritual exercises in Steps Six and Seven. And there's something about the willingness. To be willing to make amends itself requires spiritual effort. And remember, my list should include *all* those I have harmed (whether during the drinking life or before). The longer my life—not just the longer my life in drinking, though that too!—the longer will be my list. And ransacking my memory—creating a long and complete list—is likewise a spiritual exercise. And Bill W. leaves no doubt we should carry it out.

Bill W. gives us one of the primary purposes of our Eighth and Ninth Steps combined, and what the process is supposed to involve. "Steps Eight and Nine are concerned with personal relations. First, we take a look backward and try to discover where we have been at fault.... Learning how to live in the greatest peace, partnership, and brotherhood with all men and women, of whatever description, is a moving and fascinating adventure. Every A.A. has found that he can make little headway in this new adventure of living until he first backtracks and really makes an accurate and unsparing survey of the human wreckage he has left in his wake. To a degree, he has already done this when taking moral inventory, but now the time has come when he ought to redouble his efforts to see how many people he has hurt, and in what ways" (Big Book, p. 77).

These steps are about forgiveness, and particularly the willingness to make amends is about forgiveness. Here's what Bill W. says about forgiveness in the Big Book on the next page, p. 78: "The moment we ponder a twisted or broken relationship with another person, our emotions go on the defensive. To escape looking at the wrongs we have done another, we resentfully focus on the wrong he has done us. This is especially true if he has, in fact, behaved badly at all." But—he goes on to say—if "we are now about to ask forgiveness for ourselves, why shouldn't we start out by forgiving them, one and all?"

Forgiving is the key to being forgiven. Now, what *is* this forgiveness? It is (as I understand it) "to *give* completely, as an outright gift *through and through*, with no strings attached" (*per + donare* in Latin)—to renounce anger and resentment against—to pardon. That is, the person who forgives treats the person who wronged him (or her) *as though the wrong had not been done*. "Forgive and forget" are words that go together like "friends and neighbors."

What Is the Ninth Step?

Step Nine is, *Made direct amends to such people wherever possible, except when to do so would injure them or others.* "Good judgment, a careful sense of timing, courage and prudence—these are the qualities we shall need when we take Step Nine." That's from the beginning of the discussion of Step Nine in the *12 & 12* (p. 83). A tall order, you say? Yes, it is. I've been told this is a very important step and many's the time I've heard the phrase, "amends will set you free." In sponsoring women over thirty-five years, this is the step where I've received the most balking at going on—even more than with the Fifth Step—possibly because a couple of people may have fudged the Fifth Step and survived (for a while), but you can't fudge the Ninth and go on to the "broad sunlit uplands" beyond. And that means you can't fudge the Eighth.

When we make that Eighth Step list we are really doing a lot of home-work for Step Nine—reviewing just who it is we need to contact, where they are, just how to contact them. My sponsor spent a lot of time with me on this and I believe that's what made it possible for me to have such pleas-ant Ninth Step encounters. Pretty much every one I spoke to was extremely kind to me and was glad I had undertaken a new way of life— was glad I was no longer behaving the way I had for so many years. One friend said to me, "I never understood the way you were—now it's good to know it wasn't Janie, it was the alcohol—keep up the good work." It's in my story later on, in Chapter V, that there were only two people who did-n't receive me when I went to make amends, and they both were active alcoholics, my mother and my brother—they just wouldn't talk to me.

My sponsor told me to pray for them—the procedure for taking care of resentments in the story "Freedom from Bondage" in the back of the Big Book—p. 552 in the Third and Fourth editions. And to pray the Serenity Prayer. I did both. The results—if they were the results—were a long time coming, but they came. In a year and a half my brother was in touch with me, and in four years my mother also, in each case to get to an A.A. meet-ing. Was it because of my attempt to make amends earlier that they both got sober and never drank again? It certainly had something to do with it.

I got a lot of satisfaction out of making amends. I spoke to a lot of peo-ple it was right for me to speak to, to tell them I was living a new life, and as part of the process, or as a bonus to me, the opening key was turned, I think, for two of my favorite people to get sober. I call this my bonus step. I can say with very strong assurance that amends have set me free, are still setting me free. But what are amends? Or, what is amendment? It isn't just *apology*—though it can start with *apology*. Amends are made out of *remorse* for *wrong actions* and involve *reparations*—that is, *making repair* and *paying back*. Changing things for the better (like an amendment to the U. S. Constitution). Amends involve action, setting right, not just apology. And I had to be willing to stand up in front of the people I had wronged.

One of the most important of the readings at A.A. meetings is what are sometimes called the *Ninth-Step Promises*, more often simply the *Promises*. They come in a passage (from pp. 83-84 of the Big Book, concluding the discussion of Step Nine) that is frequently read either at the beginning or end of the meetings. "If we are painstaking about this phase of our development [Step Nine], we will be amazed before we are halfway through. We are going to know a new freedom and a new happiness. We will not regret the past nor wish to shut the door on it. We will comprehend the word serenity and we will know peace. No matter how far down the scale we have gone, we will see how our experience can benefit others. That feeling of uselessness and self-pity will disappear. We will lose interest in selfish things and gain interest in our fellows. Self-seeking will slip away. Our whole attitude and outlook upon life will change. Fear of people and of economic insecurity will leave us. We will intuitively know how to handle situations which used to baffle us. We will suddenly realize that God is doing for us what we could not do for ourselves. Are these extravagant promises? We think not. They are being fulfilled among us—sometimes quickly, sometimes slowly. They will always materialize if we work for them." It certainly is no accident that all these things come into our lives when we've done the first nine steps.

Amends should involve some kind of *direct* contact—"made *direct* amends"—with the person who has been harmed. Face-to-face or by telephone or by letter (or possibly by email). But as the Big Book points out, there are some who are not to be the recipient of direct amends, because those amends might harm them or others. Who are to receive these amends is to be determined by the alcoholic's sponsor, but they are to be *direct*. How are the amends to be made to those who are dead? I have been given answers ranging from prayer to writing a letter and burning it, or reading it in a graveside visit, or graveside prayer and communication with the dead. Amends are made not so much to benefit the recipient as the maker of the amends. In any case, when we make amends we make them as soon as may be possible *in our given set of conditions*. This is the Step with the expression, "first we will want to be reasonably sure we are on the

A.A. beam." It is the last of the steps concentrating on cleaning up our lives, especially our past.

What Is the Tenth Step?

Step Ten is, ***Continued to take personal inventory and when we were wrong, promptly admitted it.*** We have taken time right in the beginning of the Steps to establish our relationship with God and then we go on from there to the inventory, the confession, amends, and when we have been seriously working away at getting these things in line, we can start living today, and start living in the now. This living in the now begins with a new strength in Step Ten, where we combine taking inventory, in the form of spot check inventories, and we stand up before our friends and before God and we promptly admit our wrongdoing.

Of course it says *promptly* because, very simply, the sooner I clear away what I've done and said, the better I am, the better I feel, the closer I am to the God of our understanding. I know I have sometimes held back in making amends or apologies because I haven't wanted to make an amend to that person—*I* wasn't nearly as wrong as *they* were and *they* haven't made amends to *me*—but trying to make qualifications and excuses like these has no meaning in God's world. Their side of the street is not up to me—mine is—and I feel so much better when I keep it that way.

How do I know I need to make an amend to someone?—I get that queasy feeling in my stomach and I know I'm wrong. I resented this step for a while in the beginning because I thought, I already took inventory—I already made amends—what is this business of doing it all over again? The *12 & 12* refers to admission and correction of errors *now*! Bill W. was very wise when he wrote that. I don't know of any alcoholic (or anyone else) who benefits from carrying things around—resentments and anger and grudges and gripes. One of the benefits of this step is learning to develop self restraint. I've mentioned my temper—my throwing things (like prayer-books at my husband)—you know, after you apologize for certain acts a few times you're not so likely to repeat them. Bill W. and Dr. Bob both talked about restraint of tongue and pen—I never had any of that till I started to try to practice this step. I'm still not a complete winner on this but I'm better—we have to remember that everyone is a little emotionally off, but when I make amends they don't tend to be highly judgmental of me—if they're self-aware. And if they're not, well, that's not my side of the street. And besides (and this is one of the hardest places in the *12 & 12*—on p. 90), "It is a spiritual axiom that every time we are disturbed, there is something wrong with *us*."

The important thing in the Big Book is that Step Ten is in part a single-day version of Steps Four and Five—inventory and sharing it with someone else—and this is necessary for the maintenance of the alcoholic's spiritual condition. And the Big Book makes it very clear that this Step is about alcohol, from which there is a daily reprieve based on our spiritual condition. In the *12 & 12* a set of "spiritual exercises" are laid out in some detail—the various types of inventory-taking—the spot-check inventory, taken any time of day—the end-of-day inventory—the periodic inventory with the sponsor or spiritual adviser—the annual or semi-annual house-cleaning.

"We can try to stop making unreasonable demands upon those we love. We can show kindness where we had shown none. With those we dislike we can begin to practice justice and courtesy.... Whenever we fail any of these people, we can promptly admit it ... When in doubt we can always pause, saying 'Not my will, but Thine, be done.' And we can often ask ourselves, 'Am I doing to others as I would have them do unto me—today?' When evening comes ... many of us draw up a balance sheet for the day.... As we glance down the debit side of the day's ledger, we should carefully examine our motives in each thought or act that appears to be wrong ... Having so considered our day ... and having searched our hearts with neither fear nor favor, we can truly thank God for the blessings we have received, and sleep in good conscience" (*12 & 12* pp. 93-94). In short, every time the alcoholic finds himself with a problem (especially an unexpected problem), the first thing to do is self-examination. The same thing is true in a moment of success. The problems should be the occasion for the alcoholic's being less demanding, more kind, more just, more courteous, realizing all human beings are fallible.

The alcoholic should promptly admit error, also should say frequently "Not my will, but Thine, be done," and practice self-examination in light of the Golden Rule. "All this should become habitual. And at the end of the day, there should be a more searching self-examination, with thankfulness to God for blessings bestowed." Of course, it hurts to admit we're wrong. But we've all heard "no pain no gain" and that pain is "the touchstone of all spiritual growth" (that's from Bill W., *12 & 12*, pp. 93-94).

I'll end with this line from an old friend of mine in Blue Bell, Pennsylvania, written in my *12 & 12* under Step Ten (p. 91), about restraint of tongue and pen. "If you're wrong, promptly admit it—if you're right, shut up!"

What Is the Eleventh Step?

The Eleventh Step is, *Sought through prayer and meditation to improve our conscious contact with God* as we understood Him, *praying only for knowledge of His will for us and the power to carry that out.*

PRAYER: For me, as for many alcoholics in the early days of sobriety, prayer was not super-easy. But most of us—certainly most of us in my generation—grew up knowing about prayer either from Sunday School or our parents or church and we can latch onto something from our childhood. (Recent research on the brain has indicated that early patterns of neurotransmission—early patterns of thought, brain processes developed early on in our lives, if you like—can be re-accessed after quite a long time and brought back into use more easily than entirely new patterns can be created.) I mentioned earlier that my religious training had been cut short very early and so I came to A.A. with great distrust and even disbelief regarding a Higher Power. But the early patterns were there, I think, underneath, and my years in Alcoholics Anonymous have made it possible to get back to them.

Sometimes people ask their sponsors what they do for prayer and meditation. This was where a sponsor was indispensable for me at the beginning. She gave me a simple prayer to use—the Serenity Prayer that we've already mentioned—and she made it very clear to me that I didn't have to believe anything *yet!*—all I had to do was say the prayer. "Just do it!" she told me. My belief was not required—only hers was. Much to my amazement I found little periods of different thinking coming in. And, most important, the desire to drink disappeared. People told me this was what was called "Fake it till you make it!"

It worked for me when I believe nothing else would have. And I found myself reading that Serenity Prayer she taught me about even when I didn't have to—and the Third Step prayer, and the Seventh Step prayer—and I fell in love with the Saint Francis Prayer. All this from the sponsor who told me *I* didn't have to believe anything. I've known other people with very similar experiences—starting out on the dark side but slowly coming around into the sunshine.

MEDITATION: It's the book we call the *12 & 12* that has what is for me the best description in A.A. literature of how to get into meditation—I don't think it's original with A.A. but that's where I found it. After quoting the Saint Francis Prayer the book says on p. 100:

> As though lying upon a sunlit beach let us relax and breathe deeply of the spiritual atmosphere with which the grace of this prayer surrounds us.

That is meditating. Myself, I more often use a mantra (a short passage repeated and repeated) rather than the Saint Francis Prayer as a lead-in to meditation, chiefly because of the length of that prayer. But Bill and many others have used it. Here's the prayer, in its form in the *12 & 12* (p. 99):

> Lord, make me a channel of thy peace—that where there is hatred, I may bring love—that where there is wrong, I may bring the spirit of forgiveness—that where there is discord, I may bring harmony—that where there is error, I may bring truth—that where there is doubt, I may bring faith—that where there is despair, I may bring hope—that where there are shadows, I may bring light—that where there is sadness, I may bring joy. Lord, grant that I may seek rather to comfort than to be comforted—to understand, than to be understood—to love, than to be loved. For it is by self-forgetting that one finds. It is

by forgiving that one is forgiven. It is by dying that one awakens
to Eternal Life. Amen.

For me, it's a wonderful prayer to pray, but not so good as a lead-in to
meditation, but that's just my experience. I do better with a short repeated
mantra, as I said, or with pictures in my mind, like an arbor or trellis with
roses growing.

Some people have difficulties with meditation, as I did. I sponsor
women who tell me "I can't meditate—my brain won't slow down—morning or evening I simply cannot do it!" I tell them what was told to me,
"These Steps were written for all alcoholics, and if we persist, they will
work for us too." As I said, I've found it helps to practice meditation with
someone who is experienced. In fact we had a group which met regularly
at our house not too long ago—people who met to meditate together—
and some of them moved on to being able to meditate alone. I have found
with meditation that it seems for a while as though nothing is happening,
but sometime later on during the day an intuition will come to me or a
feeling of great peace will wash over me.

In the promises, when it says we're going to know a new freedom and a
new happiness—that we will comprehend the word serenity and we will
know peace—I believe that comes from meditation. And I am sure that
the promise "we will intuitively know how to handle situations that used
to baffle us" is directly linked to meditation.

It does say in the Big Book that we should pray and meditate "upon
awakening"—it was very strongly suggested to me that "upon awakening"
does not mean after I've had a shower, had my coffee, let the dog out, handled two phone calls—it means before anything new has come into my
experience that day. It was represented to me that "upon awakening" was
very important, and the other thing that was represented to me was the
importance of starting the day with gratitude—an "attitude of gratitude"—because I don't have to ask for sobriety when I wake up with it. I
was instructed to thank God for my sobriety first thing—to have and keep
that attitude of gratitude. Not pleading—thanking!

Bill W. suggests (Big Book p. 87) that we "should conclude the period
of meditation with a prayer that we be shown all through the day what our

next step is to be, that we be given whatever we need to take care of such problems. We ask especially for freedom from self-will, and are careful to make no requests for ourselves only.... If circumstances warrant, we ask our wives or friends to join us in morning meditation. If we belong to a religious denomination which requires a definite morning devotion, we attend to that also. If not members of religious bodies, we sometimes select and memorize a few set prayers which emphasize the principles we have been discussing." Bill W. wrote a prayer which he and Lois used in their morning prayer and meditation for many years. It's in *"Pass It On": The Story of Bill Wilson and How the A.A. Message reached the World* (New York, 1984) p. 265:

> Oh Lord, we thank Thee that Thou art, that we are from ever-lasting to everlasting. Blessed be Thy holy name and all Thy benefactions to us of light, of love, and of service. May we find and do Thy will in good strength, in good cheer today. May thy ever-present grace be discovered by family and friends—those here and those beyond—by our Societies throughout the world, by men and women everywhere, and among those who must lead us in these troubled times. Oh Lord, we know Thee to be all wonder, all beauty, all glory, all power, all love. Indeed, Thou art everlasting love. Accordingly, Thou hast fashioned for us a destiny passing through Thy many mansions, ever in more discovery of Thee and in no separation between ourselves.

This prayer, written around 1941, might be considered Bill W.'s own Eleventh Step prayer, before he borrowed an older prayer for the *12 & 12*.

Just as Step Ten suggests spot-check inventory, Step Eleven suggests spot-check prayer (Big Book pp. 87-88). This is important. We don't pray just in the morning only, but any time during the day when we become upset or anxious.

And one other thing: the *12 & 12* makes it clear that one of the things to be relaxed in prayer is one's insistence on defining the terms of the problem (*12 & 12* p. 102): "Our immediate temptation will be to ask for specific solutions to specific problems, and for the ability to help other people as we have already thought they should be helped. In that case, we are asking God to do it *our* way." And two pages further along (*12 & 12* p. 104), Bill W. gives us another warning: "We form ideas as to what we think God's will is for other people ... and we pray for these specific things. Such prayers, of course, are fundamentally good acts, but often they are based upon a supposition that we know God's will for the person for whom we pray"—so that side by side with the prayer there is presumption and conceit in the person praying. That's another thing we have to be careful about.

What Is the Twelfth Step?

The Twelfth Step is, *Having had a spiritual awakening as the result of these steps, we tried to carry this message to alcoholics, and to practice these principles in all our affairs.* It may not look it but Step Twelve is actually a three-parter, with the first part talking about "having had a spiritual awakening," and describing it as coming about "as THE result of these steps." That says to me that this is what we're aiming for—a spiritual awakening—and it tells me how it happens.

It comes into our experience *as THE result of these steps.* That is, it comes after we've learned about the importance of the Higher Power (Step Two) and have learned that this Higher Power must be given the care of our lives and our will (Step Three). After establishing a life involving the Higher Power we need to learn the importance of an inventory and how to conduct an inventory (Step Four), and that the results of that inventory—telling our stories and talking about our lives (Step Five)—are the personal knowledge we learn to share with God and another human being (and ourselves). We use all of our humility in asking to be relieved of these defects of character (Steps Six and Seven). We figure out all the people we need to contact for amends and then we contact them, making amends to everyone on our list (Steps Eight and Nine). We learn about spot check inventories and we learn the importance of admitting our wrongs done to others *promptly* (Step Ten). Then we come up to prayer and meditation every day of our lives without fail (Step Eleven)—and then we look at this list of steps we have done and see that this is what brought us to this spiritual awakening. This is how we got there—no, not there!—*here!*—*here* where we are in our spiritual awakening as the result of these steps.

All the same steps are used to establish the principles we are living by and our practicing them in all our affairs—not just at an A.A. meeting, but at home, in a job, in the community—and then (in Step Twelve) we're at the point that A.A. is famous for. We carry the message to the alcoholic who still suffers—we take phone calls, speak at meetings, take meetings into prisons—do whatever we are asked to do—like the morning Kathy R. called to ask me to take her to the Camden County Jail for Women and I didn't want to do it and I wasn't equipped to do it and Kathy talked me into it, just like many others have been talked into Twelfth Step calls over the years. And I know now that morning changed my life forever—I can't imagine my life without that morning with those women.

We all start out practicing these principles at meetings and in A.A. generally, and then we want to carry it to the job—to the community—to our neighbors—and then the hardest place of all, at home with those we love the most. The summary in the front of the *12 & 12* (on pages 8-9) tells us:

> Joy of living is the theme of the Twelfth Step. Action its keyword. Giving that asks no reward. Love that has no price tag. What is spiritual awakening? A new state of consciousness and being is received as a free gift.... Monotony, pain, and calamity turned to good use by practice of Steps.... Placing spiritual growth first. [Discarding both] domination and overdependence. Putting our lives on give-and-take basis. Dependence upon God necessary to recovery of alcoholics.... Outlook upon material matters changes. So do feelings about personal importance. Instincts restored to true purpose. Understanding is key to right attitudes, right action key to good living.

In the Big Book, the Twelfth Step takes an entire chapter (Chapter 7, "Working With Others," pp. 89-103). In the *12 & 12*, the chapter (pp. 106-125) is sufficiently long that many Step and Tradition meetings discuss it in two parts (frequently p. 106 to bottom of p. 115 and bottom of p. 115 to p. 125). Part of the reason for the length of the discussion in the *12 & 12* is the summary of Steps One through Eleven (pp. 107-109). But the chief part of the reason is that the communal life of Alcoholics Anonymous *is* the Twelfth Step: the working with others, and the carrying on from day to day as a member of the fellowship. The summary is on page 164 of the Big Book at the end of the last chapter, "A Vision for You," sometimes read at the end of meetings.

> God will constantly disclose more to you and to us. Ask Him in your morning meditation what you can do each day for the man who is still sick. The answers will come, if your own house is in order. But obviously you cannot transmit something you haven't got. See to it that your relationship with Him is right, and great events will come to pass for you and countless others. This is the Great Fact for us.
>
> Abandon yourself to God as you understand God. Admit your faults to Him and to your fellows. Clear away the wreckage of your past. Give freely of what you find and join us. We shall be with you in the Fellowship of the Spirit, and you will surely meet some of us as you trudge the Road of Happy Destiny. May God bless you and keep you until then.

CHAPTER IV

Where Can I Go for Help?

PART ONE

A.A. AND OTHER ANSWERS

So I may be an alcoholic—I want to be sober (or at least I think, maybe, just possibly, it might be a good idea to do something about my drinking)—and it looks like maybe the Twelve Steps could be part of an answer. But I don't know. Where can I choose to go for help? The operative word in the question as stated is *choose*. The place *I* went was A.A. (Alcoholics Anonymous), originally because that's where my non-drinking husband took me. Some people go to a "detox" (detoxification) facility, for starters. Some go to "rehabs" (rehabilitation facilities or treatment facilities)—I've worked at some of them since then, and many of them have done really good work, but on the whole I'm dubious. Some alcoholics or problem drinkers get their counseling in jail or prison—the only thing is, that's not ordinarily among the approaches we *choose* from.

Some go for counseling or some to psychiatrists. Some go for "IOP" (Intensive Outpatient) therapy, some seek out psychologists, and some have them provided by Employee Assistance Programs. All of these can be—and many times they are—combined with going to A.A., even for those in jail or prison. And then there are what some people call "A.A. substitutes," like "Christian Victory" or "Sisters in Sobriety," including groups like "Rational Recovery" and "Moderation Management." There is also the Church of Christ, Scientist, which advertises recovery in "One Step, Not Twelve"—which might be called an "A.A. substitute" (although, since Christian Science is in fact the older alternative, I doubt if most Christian Scientists would like this way of looking at the matter). You may choose to take your drinking problem to a physician. Some people are comfortable in the hands of a psychiatrist. Some go to a clergyman.

A.A. was my answer, originally (apparently) simply because that's where my husband took me in 1969, and where I took myself in 1970. In 1970, I asked the lady I had called on October 6th to be my A.A. sponsor (that's the morning when I didn't call the liquor store or my friend Kelly). She said she didn't think she should take on any more pigeons because she was not well. I told her, "You have to—I'm a bad case and you have the most experience of anyone around here—and I'm not leaving here without a sponsor." Finally she agreed, and told me "A step meeting every week, and as many other meetings as you can get to." This was October 6, 1970—my "date of last drink" was October 5—and now, more than 12,850 sober days and more than 7,000 meetings later, I still go to a step meeting every week, even though we had to found a step group in my present home town to do it. In Chapter V, I will be giving you something of my history as a sober alcoholic over a period of thirty-five years, and maybe I'll be needing to "interpret" it a little. It's hard to get things into the right order for this book, but right now we'll look at some of the other ways or institutions— besides A.A.—for getting sober, separately or in combination.

Nevertheless, the fundamental treatment for alcoholism in the United States has come to be some version of the Twelve Steps of Alcoholics Anonymous. Or at the very least, some cognitive process that is supposed to re-direct lives in much the same way.

What are other answers?

Other answers, as I mentioned, include "rehabs" (rehabilitation centers, with what is called "detox"—that is, a detoxification process—as the usual first stage), IOP (intensive outpatient treatment, sometimes with detox in a rehab facility first), traditional psychiatry, counseling, group therapy of various kinds and models, and even other fellowships or groups besides Alcoholics Anonymous.

Sometimes your physician may recommend that you begin with detoxification, generally a non-medical procedure lasting about three days, where you are given rest, good meals on a regular basis, and light counseling. Some "detoxes" (detoxification facilities) will allow an A.A. member to stop in for thirty to forty-five minutes for a visit to give a little reassurance and let you know what you have to look forward to. It doesn't seem as though as many people are going to detoxes now as used to go—but in the area where I live detox facilities did not start up until the mid- to later 1970s, and if you think about it, what did people do before that? I was detoxed at home as were many others before the mid-'70s.

In the early days, detoxification took place either at home or in the hospital (if you could find a hospital that took alcoholics). Sometimes now, as sometimes then, detoxification as a separate specific step toward sobriety is necessary. Snakes crawling up the walls don't seem to be as common as they used to be, although apparently some people still do see bugs and snakes—but in any case, DT's are not the only sign detoxification is necessary. The early members of A.A. detoxed their "prospects" by judicious administration of small amounts of alcohol, decreasing over time, and in some cases with a strange concoction of sauerkraut, stewed tomatoes, and Karo syrup to clean out the system and restore sugar levels.

In 1970, I was detoxed at home with no such concoction, but I had to be watched carefully. After all I had drunk a fifth of Scotch whisky every day for fifteen years (even though I kept on telling myself all those years that this was all right because it was lower in "fusel oil content" than some other forms of beverage alcohol). Detoxification may well be required before the alcoholic can begin to function well enough to make any decisions. Rehabs generally provide detoxing as a matter of course, and hospitals provide it with hospital-run IOP programs.

Later on, after I had already gotten sober, rehab centers—where a person can go to "live-in" for two to four weeks—joined detoxes as a popular step for treating alcoholism. The decision to go to a rehab is often made with the help of a physician or family members. There are a couple of different kinds of treatment used in rehab centers—one is "one on one" treatment with a therapist, who is sometimes called an addictions counselor—and then there is group treatment which involves everyone there getting together to learn about the disease of alcoholism and how it has affected them and the others in the group. (As I understand it, this more recent kind of group treatment session isn't the same thing as the "group therapy" that was practiced in the 1940s and 1950s. That was before my time, but not before my first sponsor's time.)

When the period of treatment in the rehab is over, you return to your home, and go to A.A. in your community—with a sponsor, a home group, and meetings (I believe that one of these weekly meetings ought to be the kind of A.A. meeting that is called a "step" meeting). The rehab is usually paid for through insurance or through an EAP (employee assistance program) at your place of employment. If neither of these is available, remember (as with detoxes), before they came into being, we had A.A., and people got sober without rehabs. I have sponsored people who thought they needed to be "rehabbed" or have a hospital stay to validate the fact that their alcoholism was a disease. This was never my case—I knew I was sick—and in a way, in talking about this, I'm playing my short suit. I never had things like detox facilities, rehabs, or IOP, and never felt I needed them to be either successful or even comfortable in my sobriety. I continue to believe that what is needed is increased bonding in your local A.A., with a sponsor and a home group. You have to remember that I firmly believe that the best treatment for anyone suffering the disease of alcoholism comes from following the A.A. program as set out in the Twelve Steps of Alcoholics Anonymous.

And this especially comes to mind for me when people inquire about IOP (intensive outpatient therapy). IOP is a program where you remain in your own home and go several times a week for a few weeks to lectures on alcohol—group "therapy" sessions (two or three times a week), and individual counseling (usually once a week). Sometimes I think these programs dilute what A.A. has to offer, in two ways—they don't do it as well and they take time away from A.A.'s time (their sessions crowd out A.A. meetings on the alcoholic's schedule). Since the best treatment for the alcoholic is A.A., anything that takes him or her away from the local A.A. meeting may be counterproductive. We need the relationship with a sponsor and members of the group in our area, step meetings, and speaker meetings, and we need these on a very timely basis, early and often.

Private counseling—which may be offered by psychiatrists, psychologists, and addictions counselors—can sometimes offer help for alcoholics. Unfortunately, in my experience, counseling is frequently offered when the alcoholic is extremely newly sober and unable to utilize the help that is offered. Newly sober alcoholics are often very fuzzy and their ability to assess their life situations may be limited and the assessment inaccurate. When newly sober, the alcoholic is often quite paranoid—there used to be a diagnosis, "alcoholic paranoia"—and that paranoia severely limits the ability to utilize what the counselor has offered. Perhaps this kind of counseling can best be taken advantage of once the alcoholic has some good sobriety time under the belt. I know sometimes my thinking here is considered controversial, but I've seen counseling to work best when the counseling is not provided until the alcoholic has some sobriety time already accrued.

Alcoholics Anonymous is not referred to as group therapy but many people think it offers the same benefit as "group therapy," as that is generally understood. Think about it, a group of people in a room talking about their problems with alcohol—if you're an alcoholic like I'm an alcoholic, the very best opportunity for this kind of group therapy is at an A.A. meeting.

Some years ago the practice of group therapy was developed by Dr. Harry Stack Sullivan, and in its original form, it was heavily controlled by the doctor. In A.A. we are not set up or controlled by a doctor—our meetings are bound by the group conscience of all of the people in the group, and the chairman of the meeting is a kind of facilitator, frequently a totally "hands-off" facilitator. If the group therapy you're looking for is *this* kind, then go to A.A. And it has other advantages: (1) it's an A.A. meeting so you're getting to a meeting and (2) there's no charge.

What about non-A.A. groups?

Many of us are aware that A.A. became hugely successful in aiding people to deal with the serious difficulties in their lives. Alcoholics for the first time were getting sober and staying sober and leading productive lives: they were getting back with their families, and sometimes their employers took them back. Other sufferers saw this great success of ours—narcotics addicts, compulsive gamblers, compulsive overeaters, sex and love addicts, habitual criminals, and cocaine users—and they thought they would borrow what we had, and they did just that. They took our Twelve Steps, our meeting ideas, our idea of sponsorship, and they put them to work for their addictions too, so today we have N.A., G.A., O.A., S.L.A.A., C.A., and many other groups of people who are trying to live the same lives we are in A.A. by employing our A.A. spiritual program. Everyone can find his or her way to the right group, or even groups.

On the other hand, there are other groups formed who don't want to apply the principles of A.A.'s spiritual program, or don't believe in its goals, or who want to be more inclusive, or to specialize, and we have a number of these on the horizon now. One was called Rational Recovery, which didn't think a spiritual life was to be found through belief in a Higher Power, but that is now departed—my friend Bill White, who is the leading historian on addictions treatment in this country, tells me they aren't any RR meetings any more. It has been to some extent replaced by SMART Recovery®, which was created as an alternative to both Alcoholics Anonymous and Narcotics Anonymous, and now sponsors more than three hundred face-to-face meetings around the world, and around twenty online meetings per week—and by LifeRing Secular Recovery, which was originally established as a publishing company in California in 1997. Another type of group (where the goal is not total abstinence) is Moderation Management.

A complete list of group-based recovery programs would include Al-Anon Family Groups, Alcoholics Anonymous, Alcoholics Victorious, Cocaine Anonymous, Families Anonymous, Grief Recovery After Substance Passing (G.R.A.S.P.), Heroin Anonymous, J.A.C.S., LifeRing Secular Recovery, Marijuana Anonymous, Millati Islami, Moderation Management,

Narcotics Anonymous, Nicotine Anonymous, Secular Organization for Sobriety, SmartRecovery®, and Women for Sobriety. (Obviously, Cocaine Anonymous, Heroin Anonymous, Nicotine Anonymous, and a couple of the others are pretty much beyond the scope of this book.)

In addition, there are groups called Depression and Bi Polar Support Alliance, Double Trouble in Recovery, Dual Recovery Anonymous, Emotions Anonymous, Gamblers Anonymous, Gam Anon Family Groups, GROW, Inc., the National Schizophrenia Foundation, Overcomers Outreach, and Recovery, Inc. There are also Internet-based mutual help groups: the Online Intergroup of Alcoholics Anonymous, Advocates For the Integration of Recovery and Methadone, Inc. (AFIRM), Deaf and Hard of Hearing 12 Step Recovery Resources, Methadone Anonymous Support, Sober 24, SoberDykes Hope Page, Bi Polar Disorder/Harbor of Refuge, Bi Polar Significant Others, Bipolar World, Depressed Anonymous, and Dissociative Identity Disorder. And there are what Ernie and Linda Faris Kurtz call "potentially emerging new mutual help resources": the 12 Step Pagans, Anonymous One, Clean/Sobriety for Free and for Fun, and Crystal Meth Anonymous.

Most of these are beyond the scope of this book—though a very few alcoholics I have known have had their primary recovery in Overeaters Anonymous or Narcotics Anonymous or one or two of the others.

One controversial A.A. member I know, sober for more than fifty years, has long advocated Recovery, Inc. (a cognitive behavioral mental health group founded in 1937 by neuropsychiatrist Abraham A. Low, M.D., of the University of Illinois Medical School) in combination with going to A.A. "Father John Doe," who wrote the Golden Books—widely used in A.A. when I came in and still used in the Midwest—was an advocate of Recovery, Inc., especially for those alcoholics who were particularly subject to panic attacks, unreasonable fears, and extreme perfectionism (I believe all alcoholics are subject to these in some degree). Also, Father Ed Dowling, who was for nearly twenty years Bill W.'s spiritual advisor, was likewise an advocate of Recovery, Inc.

These programs all have their own policies and their own successes (though I come across them in or around Alcoholics Anonymous only infrequently). In my own experience (and the experience of those I have known), deep change has come from "spiritual" programs, not rational behavior management, and not, by the way, from medicine (though that, of course, could change).

What about medications?

About medicine: this is one of the touchiest areas of all in dealing with the alcoholic. Remember this—Bill W. tells us that our minds and bodies are different from those of our fellows. Some alcoholics are extremely sensitive to any medication—by sensitive I mean they can have difficulty with their thoughts, difficulty driving vehicles, difficulty running their lawnmower or weedwhacker. I myself cannot take antidepressants because they build in me a desire to drink. Some alcoholics go in the other direction and seem to require more of just about anything than anyone else. Another difficult area for alcoholics is the area of surgery and anesthesia. I understand that anesthesiologists really want to know if you've ever had a sensitivity to alcohol—they will probably watch you more carefully than they watch the nonalcoholic. Most alcoholics I know find it more comfortable to stay away from more medicines, particularly in early days of sobriety. This is an area where it's very good to remember that "easy does it!"

This may seem a long way away from "where do I choose to go for help with alcoholism?" But it's evidence that it is very difficult to treat alcoholism with medication, because alcoholics often react to medicine in ways very different from "normal" reaction. It's long been a hope to find a medical treatment for alcoholism. Fully fifty years ago there was Antabuse, and it's still used, though then (and even now) it's highly controversial. Antabuse is designed to make you sick if you drink alcohol, and it's been given to people the doctors think may not be able to stay sober without it. The other side of the coin is, if they can't stay sober without it, how can they be sure to stay sober with it? When drinkers try to drink over Antabuse, the results are apt to be dizziness, severe headache, and vomiting at the least, and sometimes people have died. Obviously, any change brought about by Antabuse is in the nature of modulation—"surface" change, you might say. It isn't toward deep structural change in the brain.

I don't know if the same is true with the "anti-craving" drug Naltrexone, though the only (very limited) experience I have with A.A.s taking the drug suggests that it can be used as a "bridge-the-gap" drug to aid those discharged from rehabs in getting safely into A.A. The change Naltrexone makes—interrupting the "craving" circuits with an "anti-craving" drug— also seems to be what is called modulation, not deep structural change. As I understand the neurobiology involved, certain chemical entities increase levels of certain neurotransmitters outside the cells, thus inducing sensations of greater pleasure. In alcoholics in general, alcohol produces a greater endorphin response than it does in non-alcoholics (but their baseline level is lower). Alcohol thus increases opioid activity more in alcoholics than it does in non-alcoholics. Naltrexone is an opioid receptor antagonist—that is, it blocks the reception of those increased opioids which the alcohol produces. For those alcoholics who are genetically particularly sensitive to dopamine neurotransmission, it follows that both opioid activity and cue-related craving for alcohol could be reduced by Naltrexone, so long as the alcoholic continues to take Naltrexone.

However drinking based on greater opioid/endorphin effects is only one part of the biochemical picture. Stress increases drinking in some alcoholics (and some non-alcoholics or "situational" alcoholics). Some alcoholics have their "pleasure-counters" out of whack (this is called *hedonic dysregulation*). There is no acceptable medicine just now for stress-induced craving or hedonic dysregulation. Exaggerated frontal-area metabolism (hypofrontality) in the brain is tied to cue-induced (thus memory-induced) craving, which is one of the things that make it difficult for an alcoholic to stop after the first drink. There are some studies suggesting that Naltrexone can have a favorable effect here also. These same studies suggest that Naltrexone will work best for alcoholics who are also at risk for heroin addiction. This isn't part of any usual set of alcoholic "types"—but it does bring us back to the idea that there are different types of alcoholics.

The research on Naltrexone has come out of the University of Pennsylvania (only a hundred miles away from my home), so Naltrexone is now being prescribed for alcoholics in the area where I live. There may be other current drugs for alcoholism that have not come to my attention, but a discussion of Naltrexone really puts into a nutshell the underlying issues involved in trying to treat alcoholism with medication. It modulates brain activity in useful ways for certain types of alcoholics, and unlike the old "bridge" drugs like Valium, it isn't "alcohol in a pill." It appears to work as long as it continues to be used. But if it has been recommended that you or someone you love take Naltrexone, make sure the suggestion is from someone who has made a strong study of alcoholism—ideally (in my mind), both in A.A. as the context for recovery and in neurochemistry. And above all, my advice would be, be sure that you do not rest satisfied with a continued administration of any anti-craving drug and only that, where you are not also using some form of "talk therapy" to produce the kind of structural brain change which basically alters the way you think— the kind of enormously positive changes in thinking patterns which I see as having happened in me in my years in Alcoholics Anonymous.

PART TWO

WHAT IS IT LIKE GOING TO A.A., AND WHAT DO I DO THERE?

To start with, going to A.A. is going to meetings. A meeting is an opportunity to meet with others who have the same problem you have, who have found a way up and out. It's an opportunity for you to gather together with these people and learn how to live without alcohol.

What are A.A. meetings, and why? There are two main types of A.A. meetings—closed meetings and open meetings. Closed meetings are for alcoholics only. Open meetings are open to anyone, alcoholics and non-alcoholics—sometimes people who are close to an alcoholic and may want to go for support, and sometimes students who want to learn about alcoholism (who are welcome at an open meeting). Generally, in most places, the only participants who are encouraged to speak at open meetings are alcoholics. In other words, your best friend who is there to support you, is there for silent support, not to bring up questions or concerns.

Of open and closed meetings there are several types: *Discussion meetings* are where topics concerning alcohol or alcoholism are discussed—such as relapse or getting a sponsor—how you feel, what your concerns are, talking about finding a higher power, and so on. *Step meetings* or step study meetings are discussion meetings confined to discussion of the Twelve Steps (sometimes the Twelve Traditions are also included). They usually read from the *12 & 12*, and then after the reading, everyone has an opportunity to contribute their experience with that Step or ask questions about that Step. *Speaker meetings* are where one or more persons tell their story as alcoholics and their experience in sobriety. Some people think speaker meetings are particularly important for newcomers because the newcomer has an opportunity to identify with the speaker's life before and after getting sober, and the identification "before" makes the identification "after" easier.

Anyone who is interested in the problems of alcoholism may come to an open meeting. This should not mean—as a friend in the program says—that alcoholics who can't find baby-sitters should routinely convert open meetings into Romper Rooms. But whether the meeting is closed or open, the people who speak are alcoholics. It isn't wives, boyfriends, addicts who aren't alcoholics, nursing students, or any other non-alcoholics who talk. Of course, alcoholics who are *also* wives, boyfriends, addicts, nursing students, lawyers or whatever, can all participate by virtue of the fact that they're alcoholics. You see, the key fact about what goes on at an A.A. meeting is that it's one alcoholic talking to another. (That's what makes meetings fundamentally different from counseling sessions in rehabs or IOP or wherever.)

Now what do these meetings do?—besides making it possible for me to share parts of my story and listen to others tell theirs? My brother used to say that every A.A. meeting raises our level of consciousness. It took me a while to grasp the concept, but he believed fervently that every time an alcoholic went to an A.A. meeting, somehow, someway, there was an improvement, however small, in that alcoholic's consciousness. Teddy wasn't the only one who told me this—I've heard it from other members—but he was the one I could ask questions.

I remember asking him "when did this start?" That is, in my own case, when did this "raising of consciousness" start for me? He said, "Sister, it started for you the first time you went to an A.A. meeting." I reminded him that the first five or six times I went to an A.A. meeting I didn't believe anything. He said it didn't matter—"somewhere in your consciousness you were being touched—you were getting closer to God. It had nothing to do with your intellectualizing and your thinking that you didn't get it—no matter what you were *thinking*, every meeting you attended raised your level of consciousness."

When I was able to accept this concept, when I could look at myself from the beginning to the *now*, there was no doubt of the rise in my level of consciousness. Once I could see it, it was as clear as a sunny day. Of the two of us, my brother was the intellectual—he could always look at these concepts and "get his mind around them"—I had to have someone tell me about it, then explain it to me, then explain it to me again, But once I saw it, I knew it was real and it applied to every alcoholic I ever met. Why? I think there are three reasons,

The first reason is that we identify with the other people at the meeting. That raises our consciousness. The second reason is that we hear the "sobriety" stories—the "experience, strength, and hope"—of the other members. We learn how to do it—*and how to tell our stories*. We begin to find our patterns of thought—our neurotransmission patterns—changed from "drinking patterns" to "sobriety patterns" as we reconstruct our own narrative. The third is that any group of people gathering for the same purpose can develop a "group spirit"—whether it's an A.A. meeting or a high-school football team or an elite paratrooper unit. And being part of that spirit helps raise our consciousness.

What is a sponsor, and why? I mentioned earlier (when I talked about sponsors in Chapter II) that choosing Kay H. as my sponsor was one of the smartest moves I made, and that when I chose her, she told me what would be expected of me. But I didn't tell you exactly why it was so smart and she didn't tell me about everything she wanted me to do all at once—I suppose she didn't think I could take it. I learned gradually, and what she said at the beginning was on a very basic level. You don't need to be told again that a sponsor is an experienced, sober A.A. who can guide the newcomer into the program of Alcoholics Anonymous. It might, however, be a good idea to mention that it's a good thing if your sponsor also has an active sponsor, so that you have a "grand-sponsor" you can go to for added strength and experience. It might also be a good idea—it certainly was for me then—to choose a sponsor whose own strength and experience go back a long way. Long sobriety doesn't necessarily produce a good sponsor, but long experience is long experience, and a lot of the problems that come up in my life will have come up before.

Of course, in the very old days, you didn't so much choose your sponsor as your sponsor chose you. In those very old days, the person who "sponsored" you at your first meeting was usually (although not always) your sponsor who took you through the Steps. (Actually, in order to get in the door at your first meeting, you had to have been given the Big Book to read, and been asked some tough questions to determine how committed you were. There was no such thing as meetings that were listed in the newspapers or in a printed schedule, and you just decided to go.) In those very early days, also, the Steps seem generally to have been done pretty quickly, at which point the original "sponsorship" was over.

Times have changed. Sponsorship lasts longer now. But the need for a sponsor hasn't changed.

What books can be recommended? I read and recommend the following books: First, *Alcoholics Anonymous* (A.A.'s Big Book, originally published back in 1939, now in its fourth edition), the *Twelve Steps and Twelve Traditions* (published in 1952-53), *"Pass It On"* (a life of Bill W. published in the 1980s), *Dr. Bob and the Good Oldtimers* (about A.A. in Akron and the surrounding area up till Dr. Bob's death in 1950, also published in the 1980s), *Alcoholics Anonymous Comes of Age* (a history of the years 1935-1955, published in 1958), and *As Bill Sees It* (originally *The A.A. Way of Life*, published in 1967). These are all published by Alcoholics Anonymous World Services.

Second, there is *The Language of the Heart*, published by the *Grapevine*, and the *Grapevine* itself, a monthly magazine of articles by alcoholics—it's generally excellent.

Third, there is a book, *Twenty-Four Hours a Day* (the "little black book"), designed to be used for daily meditation by alcoholics—I use this, as many alcoholics use this, every single day. It was put together in 1948 by an A.A. named Richmond W., published from his home, and circulated by the A.A. group in Daytona Beach, Florida. In 1954, publication was taken over by the Hazelden Foundation, not previously a publisher.

I sometimes use another Hazelden book, *Day by Day*, which came out of the Denver Young People's Group in 1974, and is designed to be used by both alcoholics and addicts. Also I use *As Bill Sees It*, and the Bible, and a book called *God Calling* by Two Listeners (1938), on which parts of the *Twenty-Four Hours* book are based.

What about the A.A. "Slogans" or "Sayings"?

I've looked for a way to give someone who doesn't know the flavor or "internal reality" of Alcoholics Anonymous an idea of what it's like, and I've hit on the slogans or sayings of A.A. as a way. You might say there are two kinds of mottoes or slogans or sayings in A.A. There are half a dozen that have official or semi-official status (the official are "First Things First" and "Live and Let Live" and "Easy Does It" and "But for the Grace of God"—and the "semi-official" are "Think Think Think" and "One Day at a Time" and "Let Go and Let God!"). Then there are others frequently heard when I came in to Alcoholics Anonymous and still heard now, at least where I've been, but mostly they summarize experience in A.A. rather than having their origin in A.A. literature (although "You have to give it away to keep it" is based in A.A. literature—even if it is more important in N.A. literature).

Seven "official" and "semi-official" slogans/mottoes/sayings

"First Things First" This is one of three "mottoes" given on page 135 of the Big Book as "apropos" for living a sober life in Alcoholics Anonymous. The other two are "Live and Let Live" and "Easy Does It." There isn't much to say about it that isn't obvious. One point that may be of interest—if the five plaques containing the five "slogans" are "properly" arranged, the first words should be "First Live Easy" for these three, then "But Think" for the next two. The phrase itself—"First Things First"—has origins long before Alcoholics Anonymous. An alternative saying (with much the same focus), "Do the next right thing," is often heard in A.A. now—perhaps as often as "First things first!" The much older form is simply "Do the next thing"—and that's two centuries or more older than Shakespeare, and it occurs in one of the prayers in the little black book.

"Live and Let Live" This also is pretty obvious, and it likewise has origins long before A.A., but it is not easy to trace in print, and probably not important to do that tracing. It can be found framed on the wall of many

A.A. meeting rooms along with "Easy Does It!" and "First Things First!" I don't know about others, but for me, it's a lot harder than it seems, just to live and let live—it's another version of what the popular newspaper advice column called *Dear Abby* used to say, "MYOB—Mind Your Own Business." Some people will find this as easy as pie—others find it very difficult. It means letting other people live their lives whether we think they're right or wrong, particularly when we think they're wrong—whether they bought the right house or wrong—went to the right university or not—no matter what we think, it just shouldn't matter—*to us.* (Particularly hard for parents with grown-up children.)

"Easy Does It" This also is obvious, and a well-known piece of advice before there was an A.A, and it likewise is difficult to trace in print—and probably not important to do the tracing. This also is on page 135 of the Big Book—it might be the most used of the four Big Book slogans. Like these others, it's on a plaque on the wall in most A.A. rooms, but in my thirty-five years, I've heard it more than any other slogan—looking for a job, looking for a car, looking for a new girlfriend or boyfriend, cleaning a house—chances are at least several somebodies will say (or would say) "Easy does it!" Though maybe people said it to me so much because I particularly needed (and still need) to take it easy. One frequent use has to do with making changes after you first get sober—don't do it too quickly. (I've often heard it interpreted as supporting a ban on making any significant changes in the first year of sobriety, which is advice that has become more popular since the rehabs came along.)

The five or six slogans that we often see on plaques have a certain amount of authority because they come from the early A.A. tradition—these first three, as I said, come straight from page 135 of the Big Book. They are used frequently at meetings to remind us, to bring things up to the level of conscious thought for us, and by sponsors with their pigeons—they're quick and easy—you don't have to look them up and you know they're legitimate.

"But for the Grace of God" The fourth, "But for the Grace of God," is likewise from A.A. literature, but it is a very old expression, older than Shakespeare. It also may be the most misunderstood slogan—"But for the

Grace of God" doesn't mean exactly the same thing as reminding people to call upon "the grace of God" whenever they are in difficulties—but I think the misunderstanding (if that's what it is) is only grammatical. "There but for the grace of God, go I" is the fuller version—actually it goes back 450 years to a man named John Bradford, who said, "There but for the grace of God goes old John Bradford" when they were hauling another man away to execution back 450 years ago for—among other crimes—embezzling government funds, which was something old John Bradford himself had done in his drinking days. The phrase occurs in the Big Book not as a slogan but in the discussion early on in Chapter 2 on pages 24-25: "But for the grace of God there would have been thousands more convincing demonstrations" of the way alcoholics could end up dying, going permanently insane, or being locked up for the rest of their lives. In thirty-five years I've seen countless alcoholics who apparently just could not stop—and there but for the grace of God go I. My early recovery was very difficult but I've seen a lot of people who had it a lot rougher than I did. I don't know why I was so lucky, but I know that it wasn't my effort at first—it was what I think was the grace of God that took the drink out of my hand and hasn't put it back.

I remember arguing with Kay H. about "there but for the grace of God" one day. She said it was the grace of God that kept me from going to the Roger-Wilco liquor store and stocking up on liquor that day. I protested and told her this hadn't been God. I was the one who didn't stop at Roger-Wilco! I was the one who didn't get out of the car, didn't open the trunk, didn't go in. She said to me, "I don't care what you did or didn't do, but it was the grace of God. Otherwise, why were you one day going to Roger-Wilco and the next day not going? One day buying a case of Dewar's White Label and the next day not buying anything?" She insisted that without the grace of God I would never have had my mind changed. I continued to argue, "but I was the one who didn't buy liquor." She said no, that *it was another in me*. I've heard arguments (not in A.A.) about the grace of God. But in my own experience, what was meant by the power of God's grace settled on me that last night, and I have been powerfully reminded of it since.

I saw a speaker one night when my son was an infant—I took him into the meeting with me and held him on my lap. The speaker was a man named Sam—he had gotten drunk and he was smoking a cigarette and the cigarette fell into the side of the chair when Sam passed out—it created a tremendous fire in which he lost part of his nose and face and one ear. That could have been me in that chair with a glass of Scotch whisky and a cigarette—but for the grace of God, I would have been that person without a face.

"Think Think Think" I have heard a story about Clarence S., who founded the Cleveland group of Alcoholics Anonymous, a story about the original "Think" sign, which was borrowed from IBM (the International Business Machines Corporation), where the management hung them on the walls to encourage their employees to do their jobs thoughtfully and intelligently. I heard that Clarence believed we should throw away all the "Think Think Think" signs—that to ask an alcoholic to think was asking for trouble—and here I'm inclined to agree with him. When I get around to the thinking stuff I can think myself a long way away from serenity. My sponsor, Big Book Mary, told me that when Clarence saw the "Think" sign he protested, saying "That's the last thing alcoholics are equipped to do— think!" And later, when he saw the "Think Think Think" sign he was even more perturbed, and said "That's how we really get in trouble!" I asked Mitchell K., who was one of Clarence's pigeons and who put together the Clarence S. Archive that's now at Brown, and he tells me that the IBM sign story is correct, and that Clarence always said alcoholics don't really think—they emote! But the idea of "thinking the drink through" has taken hold in Alcoholics Anonymous, and that's what seems to be behind the continuing use of "Think Think Think."

"One Day at a Time" This has been really a hard one for me to get down pat—I have always had a tendency to project into the future (with fear), so I was a very fearful person when I got sober. I was seldom able to stop my fear, my projecting, my outlining, instead of just living today. It's easier now, but it seems to me in my case it's taken a lot of practice to get down to living one day at a time. This one, by the way, is a little easier to trace back in history than some of the others—it was a well-known line

from William Lyon Phelps (1865-1943), Professor of English at Yale, licensed Baptist Minister, and "America's Favorite Professor" in the 1920s, who popularized the theme—and the saying—in his columns and sermons. It has become so widespread in A.A. that it is frequently simply abbreviated "odat" or "odaat." It was so identified with Phelps that in his *Autobiography* in 1939 he explained how he came across the idea, and how it went back to 1879. From him it was picked up by Emmet Fox, a popular New Thought preacher, and from Emmet Fox it came into A.A.

"Let Go and Let God!" For me this was one of the tough ones—I tended to be what was known as a control freak, a worrywart, someone who "outlined" everything, trying to work out detailed imaginary scenarios in my head of what *I thought* was going to happen. To let go of something, to put it out of my mind, to think "I don't have control"—that was hard. "Letting God" was harder in the early days when I didn't believe in God. Later on I wanted to work with God on it, but to let go and *let* God was really hard. Maybe it comes easily to other people—it doesn't to me. But things are much better when I do let go, and much, much better when I do both—let go myself, and then allow God to handle the problem.

Eight other old-time slogans

Some of the other phrases we hear around A.A. like "Fake it till you make it"—"Develop an attitude of gratitude"—"Amends will set you free"—"You've got to give it away to keep it"—"If you don't remember your last drink perhaps you haven't had it"—"It gets different before it gets better!"—aren't in the Big Book, but I've heard them at many meetings, and I think they can have a kind of authority. It looks to me as though they are "process of sobriety" slogans at least as much as "state of sobriety" slogans, though of course it's perfectly possible for them to be both, and I guess some of them are.

"Fake it till you make it" Funny thing, when I first heard this expression, I thought, this is really stupid—rude, unthinking, unfeeling—and then it happened to me. I suddenly realized that what I was doing—I was praying the Serenity Prayer so I wouldn't pick up a drink, and I really didn't believe

God would help me, but I prayed anyway—that *was* faking it till I made it. Now you know, I did finally learn to believe, but I don't know whether "faking it" was part of it or just kept me out of trouble till I came to believe. I still hear "fake it till you make it" and I've urged people to do it—I think it can be part of gaining sobriety. I still don't like the "fake it" (we're supposed to live a program of rigorous honesty), but it's catchy—it's accepted—and the underlying meaning is o.k. The British author C. S. Lewis called this "holy hypocrisy"—acting to seem better than you are, and so you become better than you were. When you grow into being better than you are by pretending to be better than you are, that's part of what we mean by the hidden power of the grace of God.

"Develop an attitude of gratitude." My sponsor told me every morning to thank my Higher Power for my sober day. I don't have to ask for sobriety, because I woke up sober. I don't know a lot about the religions of the world or about spirituality, but it's my understanding that living in the world comfortably requires gratitude. The story is told of a man who used to say at every meeting that we have to develop an attitude of gratitude—and even now, if you say "attitude of gratitude" there are many A.A.s who will think of that particular man. And what he said was good—I've seen a lot of people struggling to get through the daily march and an attitude of gratitude can be what makes it less a struggle and more a real march. Not just gratitude but an *attitude* of gratitude. We need to walk and talk and stand and look and listen, and *march*, with that attitude—not just being grateful when we remember to be, but having that gratitude underlying and defining everything we do. It shouldn't be something that we have to *remember*!

"Amends will set you free." I first heard that from Johnny Q. in Philadelphia (it was a very popular saying when I got sober). I had started to make some amends and his words really had an impact on me. Amends really do bring with them a sense of freedom—I really do believe that.

But, you know, I asked before about the meaning of this term "amends," and it would be a good idea to look carefully at this in order to understand that slogan. What are they? The Eighth and Ninth Steps are the amends steps, and we talk about amends there. When I can go to someone for something I did or said and I can tell them how much I regret that I ever did that, and know that I'm no longer that person and my prayer is that I not do that, ever again, then when I get in my car and I'm on my way home, I'm beginning to be free. As I make the amends I have listed on my list and time goes by, I become more and more free. Sometimes I'm not even aware of it at the time—I'm only aware of it later—but this is what that saying means, "amends will set you free." Free from what? It's a good question, and I can't answer for anyone else, but for me, the most noticeable thing is, free from the gnawing feeling in the pit of my stomach that you have but you don't know why you have it and it's been there so long you just think it's a part of you. And then somewhere along the way the knot in the stomach isn't as big as it used to be. I remember I had that really fierce knot and never thought it was going to go away. And after I'd made my amends I began to feel better and to sleep better. It's hard to sleep when you're carrying the weight of the world in the pit of your stomach.

Others may obtain other releases from the amends they make. Some have said it's freedom from the "bondage of self"—you make the amends out of remorse and then you're out from under the remorse, and you don't have to think about yourself any more. Others have said it's freedom from fear—you make the amends and then you don't have to duck into the next aisle at the grocery store because you see someone you hurt in your drinking days (or even before—we don't just make amends to those we hurt while drinking). Still others have said it's freedom from anger—anger that's inside us and comes out because it can't stay in, not because of what anyone did to us. I'm sure all of these are right—but for me it's freedom from the gnawing anxiety and the physical pain that used to be called heartache. (I don't mean I'm not heartsick sometimes and my heart doesn't ache sometimes, but it's not from something in the unforgiven past—it's from something happening now.)

"You've got to give it away to keep it." This is from the Big Book (sometimes used with the addition of "You can't give away what you don't have"). It comes into our Twelfth Step. When we go on a Twelfth-Step call or take a drunk call in the middle of the night from the hotline, when we

pick someone up and take them to a meeting, when we stay after a meeting to talk to someone crying her heart out and even if we have a hot date on the other side of town we stay and listen, when we speak at a meeting with no advance notice because the first speaker didn't show up, when they need someone to drive the car for a trip to the prison, and when someone just came back from a slip and they think they're a hopeless case and three people have refused to sponsor them and they saw you coming and you agree, when you put money in the basket and there isn't any more where that came from, when you make a commitment to set up in the month of August and it turns out August has five Thursdays, when this is the third group that has asked you to be treasurer in five years because no one else will do it—that's all part of giving it away, and every time you give it away, you keep a little more and a little more and a little more—like small deposits in the bank, or the old Green Stamps. Stores would give you Green Stamps when you made a purchase, and when you had collected enough of them and pasted them in a little book they gave you, you could turn them in and get a prize like a toaster or a set of kitchen knives.

I mention the meditation for November 2nd in the little black book many A.A.s use in their daily meditations. "Keep yourself like an empty vessel for God to fill. Keep pouring out yourself to help others, so that God can keep filling you up with His spirit. The more you give, the more you will have for yourself. God will see that you are kept filled as long as you are giving to others. But if you selfishly try to keep all for yourself, you are soon blocked off from God, your source of supply."

"If you don't remember you're last drink perhaps you haven't had it." The first couple of times I heard this, I was puzzled. It took a while to sink in but when it did, wow!—it brought home a message that was loud and clear, that if I went around not remembering where alcohol had taken me, I could go through the whole thing again. Even though I was usually a blackout drinker, I do remember the whole night of my last drink—and I need to remember everything that happened, in order to remember where alcohol really took me when I drank, because that was a place I never want to go again.

That memory was sometimes the paramount thing in my mind which was keeping me sober. It was one piece in a puzzle which I had to solve in order to save my life, fitting in with other pieces that told me that alcoholism was incurable, fatal, and progressive. Hearing this saying brought all the other pieces of this puzzle together.

I knew I wanted that last drink on October 5, 1970, to remain my last drink—make no mistake about it, I didn't want to go back. I wasn't in love with sobriety, I didn't enjoy going to these cockamamie meetings—but I didn't want to go back where I'd been. So this is one saying—"If you don't remember your last drink, perhaps you haven't had it!"—that really had a meaning for me, because in the beginning it was the one motive for staying sober that I could understand.

"It gets different before it gets better!" I think this saying is more common in the Midwest and on the West Coast than in the East. In any case, though some may disagree with me, I view this as something good to say when things are looking really lumpy. This is just something you're going through. At a time like that it's easy and useful to tell people that it isn't going to be like this always—things will get better—because sometimes saying "this too shall pass away!" sounds a little shallow and unfeeling. "It gets different before it gets better" has a much more modern ring to it, and that can be important. Sometimes people have to ask, *What does that mean?*—and you have to tell them. And sometimes I've heard them told, *"It* is *you*—*you* have to get different before *you* get better." Which sounds to me like saying, "The same person will drink again," meaning that if you stubbornly stay the same person, you will always eventually drink again. Either way, it's a good reminder.

"Rehab" slogans heard in A.A.

"Ninety in ninety!" The most commonly heard slogans in A.A. that don't originate in A.A. are "90 in 90"—going to ninety meetings in ninety days, generally understood to require a meeting every day—along with reminders of the dangers of "people, places, and things!" (which I have also heard as "change your playground and your playmates"). Both of these came from

the rehabs in the 1970s, but they are still widely quoted. Both echo principles or sayings or tag lines that used to be heard more frequently in A.A., but that these "catchier" slogans have pretty much replaced.

"Ninety in ninety" is trying to give a short easy way to say that "what we really have is a daily reprieve contingent upon our spiritual condition" (page 85 in the Big Book). It's put in this capsule form because the first ninety days have been considered critically important and we do want people to go to meetings every day at least for that long. There's a commonly heard remark in A.A.—"My sponsor told me to do a 'ninety in ninety' and I did, and then I asked him what I should do then, and he said, 'Do another one!' And then after another 'ninety in ninety' I asked him the same question— and I got the same answer again!" (And again ... and again....) It boils down to the daily reprieve, and that's all we have—and we have to do whatever is necessary to keep that reprieve, and what is necessary is to show up every day. The slogan is easy to remember and sounds really easy to do. It's "catchier" than "we have a daily reprieve contingent upon the maintenance of our spiritual condition." This is a view going back a long way, long before Alcoholics Anonymous. I think it goes back at least to a preacher named Jonathan Edwards, two hundred and fifty years ago. He preached a famous sermon about "sinners in the hands of an angry God"—in which he said that we sinners have a daily reprieve (from being dropped from the hands of God) contingent on our continued striving.

"People, places, and things!" This is a way of saying that when you get sober, you have to change your playground and your playmates. We don't want to hang around in bars any more or sit around our best friend's kitchen table where everyone's drinking—so sobriety is time to change where we go, whom we go with, and what we do when we get there. We go to meetings with our sponsor and get there early and sit there and be quiet and we listen—and it's probably not a coincidence that I went from sitting at my best friend's kitchen table in Moorestown, New Jersey, having drinks, to sitting many nights at my sponsor's kitchen table in Mount Joy, Pennsylvania, having ice cream and cookies and cake.

It is very often suggested that we stay out of bars—certainly unless we have a good reason to be there and are in good spiritual shape. In the *12 &*

12 Bill W. talks about recovered alcoholics being able to go even to "ordinary whoopee parties." I'm not sure I could find a good reason to be there at "ordinary whoopee parties" or why I would want to be there, if I were in good spiritual shape—but that may just be my personal reaction. On the other hand, I have no objection to going to restaurants where liquor is served, though I'd prefer not to sit at the bar. Even after thirty-five years though, I wouldn't be really happy about going to a bar where I used to drink (although there aren't many left) even if it served good food.

PART THREE

FOUR MORE QUESTIONS ABOUT ALCOHOLISM AND ITS TREATMENT

Question I: How do I recognize alcoholism in someone I love? and what do I do?

If the person is a parent, same-age (or nearly same-age) sibling (and you're an adult), or any non-related person in these same age categories, you would recognize alcoholism in them pretty much the same way you would recognize it in yourself—if you knew as much about them as you know about yourself. But there are questions you need to answer.

How much do they drink? What do they drink? When do they drink? Are they getting along with others who are close to them? (Probably not, if they're drinking alcoholically.) Has anyone mentioned alcohol or alcoholism to the person in question? What was the response? (If they answered readily, "Yeah, I think I should look into that" and went off to look into it, then it's quite possible they're not alcoholic, but if they declined to do anything, if they denied there was a problem, if they were angry at "interference" or their feelings were hurt, then quite possibly they are alcoholic.) The best thing to do is to get the person in question to an A.A. meeting where they can listen and get an idea of what alcoholics are like and what A.A. is about. Have them meet A.A.s with a lot of experience and have those A.A.s answer questions for them (after or before the meeting). The next best thing, if they absolutely refuse to go to any A.A. meeting is to have them see a counselor, physician, or clergyman who has really definite good information about alcoholism and alcoholics. If they won't go to an A.A. meeting and they won't go to a doctor or counselor or clergyman, and you're still really concerned about their welfare, you may want to ask someone really close to them to help you—a sibling or friend for example—and mention what you know about alcoholism, what you've tried to do to help this person, and see what you can do to join forces to pool resources. More than likely the friend or sibling will be glad to do what they can—you can network—see who you know who knows something—see who you can come up with—and of course the great opportunity to help anyone—prayer!

It doesn't seem to matter what prayer, but prayer to some Higher Power, and a prayer that is filled with love and concern about this person. Alcoholics get well all the time and more often than not it's through the assistance and concern of someone in their lives who isn't an alcoholic. In my case it was my husband, who was a non-alcoholic and not even much of a drinker. You yourself might want to make a couple of A.A. meetings to see what goes on. Another possibility is Al-Anon—they have a lot of ideas to help you help your friend.

One really difficult problem has to do with confusion between "kids drinking" and alcoholism. There are teenagers and young adults "referred" to A.A. when they come out of rehab, where they have been sent for persistent underage drinking. Some of these may not be alcoholics (or not *yet*). Some certainly are. But this raises another question we have to ask.

Question II: Do answers that work for adults work for teenagers or younger adults?

In the year 2002 I went to a "Workshop" put on by a local division of A.A. The three speakers were men who had been sober in A.A. more than half their lives, coming in at seventeen, nineteen, and nineteen—on the Jersey shore, at a New England college, and in northern Westchester County, New York. The topic was "getting sober in your teens, and staying sober" or words to that effect. The stories were very good, so good that I almost forgot to see what they had in common. But then I looked again.

This is, of course, "only anecdotal evidence," but note this. First, the man with the longest drinking history (at nineteen), who had been on his own since his early teens, reported that his way of thinking had "just changed" at the time he came in. Second, the other man who became sober at nineteen had to be coerced by his college to go to A.A., but after a year or so, his mind changed. He had only begun drinking seriously when he went to college at eighteen—before that he hadn't wanted to drink because college was his way out of his home town—so he started late. Third, the one who got sober at seventeen came under court sentence and had been constrained to come to A.A. meetings for at least two years, when suddenly what his (much older) sponsor and the (much older) members of his group had been telling him began to make sense (and he had begun alcoholic drinking very early).

All three had family histories of alcoholism. It could, of course, be only anecdotal coincidence that the age of mind-change toward sobriety came at nineteen for the early drinkers and twenty for the later drinker. But it is exactly what we should expect, on two counts. First, nineteen/twenty is the age at which teenagers can be expected (biochemically) to stop acting so much like teenagers. Second—though we have no statistical evidence to bear any weight—it seems reasonable that earlier drinking might be connected with earlier maturity. The seventeen-year-old (1) was constrained to remain alcohol-free by the court for the next several years and (2) was able to learn how to stay sober by being in nearly constant companionship with older sober men.

Question III: What happens if we ignore warnings?

There are two kinds of warnings—the "alcoholism in others" warnings go with Question I and I'm not certain we can say much about them that we won't be saying about our own warnings. We should recap some of those warnings here—drinking more, drinking earlier in the day, drinking at the same time every day, difficulty on the job, difficulty getting along with others, difficulty driving a vehicle, maybe even getting arrested, maybe even throwing up all over—not to mention headaches, sometimes blurred vision, blackouts, difficulty getting along with friends, grandiose plans not followed through with, friends commenting about our drinking, and loved ones commenting about our drinking. When we ignore any or all of these there's a very simple rule for the outcome—jails, institutions, or death from our progressive incurable fatal disease. There are many warning signs and when they are ignored the illness gets worse and worse and worse to the point of—well, jails, institutions, or death.

I thought that was just propaganda when I first became aware of A.A. Certainly not every untreated alcoholic dies from what we think of as direct complications of alcoholism—cirrhosis of the liver or drunk driving accidents, for example. Nor do they all wind up with what used to be called "wet-brain" nor do they all act irrationally (like shooting themselves or someone else) under the force of alcohol-induced paranoia. Perhaps there should be a reformulation—the untreated alcoholic will die from complications of alcoholism, or wind up in jail or the local "twitch-farm" if he lives long enough, if he doesn't die from something else first, or if he isn't incarcerated for something else first. But an estimated 85 percent of all inmates in the State Correctional Institute where I worked had alcoholism or alcohol-related crimes or alcohol-related illnesses, in their dossier. Those who went regularly to A.A. when they got out had a chance of not coming back—it was a virtually sure bet the others would.

This I know. We speak of "jails" and "institutions" as separate entities. But the greatest number of persons being treated for rehabilitation for alcoholism in the United States are being treated in correctional institutions. It brings to mind a one-word A.A. slogan—"Yet!" I haven't gone to jail—(chorus of members) "Yet!" I haven't lost my license—(chorus of members) "Yet!" My wife hasn't divorced me—(chorus of members) "Yet!" And so on, for any "Yet" you care to mention. And of course, we all may think we're different. We stopped in time on our own (or by some other means), or we were never that bad, or it will never happen to us. We can always get through the railroad crossing before the train even if the gates are down. And you know, sometimes we can. But that doesn't prove it's the safest way home or maximizes our chances of long life.

Question IV: Is abstinence the only answer?

Generally speaking, within A.A., the answer to this question is *yes*. Partly that may be because the founders of A.A. had tried and failed to control their drinking over and over again, and weren't about to go down that road again. (That doesn't mean no one can successfully go down that road, but it is suggestive.) Partly the abstinence answer comes because abstinence is easy to measure; "normal" or "moderate" drinking is not. Let's for the moment allow that there's some kind of "normal" social drinking (at least as a goal) that doesn't involve substantially altered states of consciousness—though, as I say, for me and those other alcoholics I have talked to about this, it's pretty inconceivable.

But it's an old dream to "return" alcoholics to "normal" drinking, even though there are a lot of alcoholics who never *did* drink "normally" in the first place—for the obvious reason that their bodies don't process alcohol "normally" and alcohol doesn't act "normally" on their bodies. Does this mean alcoholics can never drink just one or two drinks and then stop? Well, never say *never*—but this seems very unlikely to me. One thing I know: I myself was never interested in normal drinking—except when I was deluding myself into believing that the kind of drinking I did *was* normal.

When I had been sober for six or seven years, a West Coast "think-tank" issued a report saying that some alcoholics could safely return to social drinking. Some alcoholics took that as official permission (so to speak) to resume drinking, and the results were not good. The report apparently had serious flaws—I can't say that for sure (it's been argued over for thirty years now)—but the think-tank was so embarrassed by some of the criticisms that it quickly withdrew the report, and tried to bury it and completely redo the research—and it's obviously true that the report's interpretation by alcoholics who were looking for permission to get back to alcohol was flawed.

Much more recently there has been a program called Moderation Management that suffered adverse publicity when its founder went back to alcoholic drinking and killed someone in a drunk driving accident. The question of course is, if there are drinkers who can reasonably seek moderation, which drinkers can moderate their drinking, and which drinkers must abstain? My friend Bill White tells me that there are successful chapters of Moderation Management around the country. Obviously, A.A. is not the place to meet successful moderate drinkers, although I'm sure Bill

White is right in saying that some such people exist. My experience with "controlled drinking" has led me to be skeptical of moderate drinking as a goal for alcoholics of my type, but *never say never!* And one thing we are learning again after forty years is that there are indeed different types of alcoholics.

When Dr. George Vaillant used his longitudinal data to find out if heavy drinkers in his samples had over time successfully returned to "normal" drinking, he found quite a few who said they had, but none that he could say for sure had done it (though there were some who might have). Dr. Vaillant does not believe there's any real value in setting out different types of alcoholics. I'm not at all sure I agree. Maybe there are rare (perhaps Jellinek beta) alcoholics or "situational alcoholics" who can learn to moderate their drinking. Certainly none of this says moderation can't be a goal. But all of it says it's proved hard to do and hard to measure. We can pretty much tell whether someone is abstinent. We can't always define "social drinking" or "normal social drinking" or "normal drinking" in any useful way. Particularly, in my experience, alcoholics can't.

CHAPTER V

My Story: Jane S. in Sobriety

PART ONE

FINGERS REACHING THROUGH THE PRISON WIRE

I came into Alcoholics Anonymous for good in October 1970. I was told back then that service, meetings, sponsorship, the fact of one alcoholic talking to another—those are the things that really help. My sponsor told me she had done it one day at a time and the "one day at a time" was explained to me this way—I would live my life emotionally one day at a time, not regret the past, not worry about the future, and if I did that, I wasn't going to have to drink again, ever. And I was told that people who went it alone did not succeed, and "service" is a very big part of the secret. I was told to stay with people who had a lot of experience. I was told, don't get sober for anybody else but yourself but learn from the sobriety of others. I wasn't exactly sure what the people who told me these things were talking about. I was told the two key words were "love" and "service" (I found out later that these were the two words that one of A.A.'s co-founders used to describe the basis of the program of Alcoholics Anonymous).

On the question of service: my group in South Jersey wasn't sure that washing coffee cups and cleaning ashtrays was enough service for me, with my shaky sobriety (that was back when they had smoking meetings and no

78

disposable Styrofoam cups), so they created a new service position, Group Librarian. The last Tuesday of the month was Anniversary Night, and the Group Librarian's responsibility was to keep track of the anniversaries. So I kept track of anniversaries, and on Anniversary Night there would be a sheet-cake with everyone's name on it who had celebrated an anniversary that month. That was my beginning in service. I had to ask every member of the group when his or her sobriety date was (that member's "Date of Last Drink"). I was the member who came late, sat in the back of the room, didn't open my mouth, and didn't want to meet anyone. I had all these names down on pieces of paper and I stuffed them in my tote bag and I had a notebook—I didn't know what to do, list by anniversaries or list by members, so after some moments of panic, and calling my husband, I decided how to do it. In the first half of the book I listed anniversaries alphabetically by name and in the second half by anniversary month. It was a great book and it served the purpose of getting me to talk to other members.

The big anniversary was the ninety-day anniversary. The ninety-day pins were very small gold pins in the shape of a triangle and at the top of the triangle was a pointed capital *G*. At the opposite corners of the triangle at each corner was an *A*. The top of the *G* made the point (apex) of the triangle. In the center of the triangle was a raised dot. There were no chips or medallions then in South Jersey, but ninety-day pins were presented in front of the group, by your sponsor, on the ninetieth day. The *G* was for *God*, the two *A*s for *A.A.*, and the dot was for you—as long as you stayed between God and A.A. you would always be well.

Then my sponsor asked if I'd made a decision about myself—after ninety days of sobriety, was I going to return to my previous life, or was I going to stay with sobriety? I and everyone else I ever heard said we were going to stay with sobriety. I don't know if pins like that are still used, but I still have mine. It was a small unassuming pin—actually a stud you could put into a button hole. The ninety-day pin was not sponsored by A.A., but, just like the chips and medallions today, was provided by an independent provider.

The moment my sponsor asked me what my decision was, I actually didn't know. I couldn't think that far ahead for anything that important, but I was terrified to say that. I was afraid everyone would think me a dummy, so I said I was going to continue on this path. It was like being sworn into a secret society, or being accepted as a candidate for knighthood, or something like that. I was trembling and red with blushing and nervousness and really frightened when I sat down, and told myself I was going to take the Scarlett O'Hara approach, and think about all that tomorrow. But my answer to my sponsor was prophetic. I'm still a member of that society now, thirty-five years later.

My first exposure to A.A. in 1969 had been about six meetings in Moorestown, New Jersey—six meetings (there might have been seven) where I was unable to identify as an alcoholic, where I came as late as I could, and left as early as I could, and just wanted to get out of there. Whatever my problems were (and I didn't think they were as bad as my husband did), I knew a group of drunks just couldn't help me—the best psychiatrists had already failed. And I didn't exactly get to A.A. on my own. It wasn't my idea. I was at the shore with my two stepdaughters and my mother, and I was to pick up my husband at the Philadelphia airport. I never arrived at the airport, and to this day I have no idea where I went: I simply forgot I was supposed to pick him up. When he got down to the shore, I was out somewhere with my brother. I had left the children in my mother's care—my mother who was a serious alcoholic—and my husband was furious.

My trip to the shore was cut short—very short, immediately, and not by me. When we got home, my husband called A.A.—the South Jersey Intergroup—and they asked if he would put his wife on the phone. I got on the phone and the person on the other end asked me if I had a drinking problem. I told them I didn't know, but my husband thought I did. They asked me my first name and phone number. Within twelve minutes I had a call from the lady who eventually (a year later) became my first sponsor. (It turned out she lived within sight of my house.) But you know, as far as I was concerned, I wasn't like these people. Or not yet!

It was suggested I try controlled drinking (I found out later this business of "controlled drinking" was in the Big Book of Alcoholics Anonymous). The idea was to drink two drinks a day (no more, no less) for six months, and if you could do this without increasing the amount of alcohol you consumed, you probably weren't an alcoholic. I however increased my amount to a full bottle of Dewar's White Label Scotch Whisky a day, on the very first day I tried it (actually I started on the bottle that night after the meeting). It was obvious to anyone—except me—that I was an alcoholic, but I went on drinking this way for another year. Also, I began to lie about my drinking (hadn't done that), hide my bottles (I hadn't done that before) and disappear from home to drink in peace (I hadn't done that before either). At the end of the year I finally came back to Alcoholics Anonymous. I'm telling you this because my experience isn't just my experience: it links with the experience of others who've come to A.A. (and many who haven't), and because telling my story is part of what keeps me sober. We'll get to that later on.

My last drinking weekend began on Friday, October 2, 1970. I drove to the liquor store and bought a bottle of Dewar's White Label Blended Scotch Whisky. I left my car somewhere, I don't remember where (I think it was in New Jersey), and I went to a motel. I don't remember taking a taxi to get there but I must have. I do remember I took a taxi to get home, so I probably took one to get there. All night I drank, smoked cigarettes (Salem Premium Length that I carried in my big white tote bag big enough for a fifth, and six packs of cigarettes, and my make-up), and I had a yellow pad where all night I wrote down the heartaches of my life. (Later on I used that yellow pad to write down my life story for my sponsor, which sounds like almost the same thing, but there's a whole wide difference in attitude.)

Saturday around noon I got a taxi home and I walked into the kitchen where my husband, two children (my two step-daughters, ages thirteen and four), and the dog were seated around the kitchen table having lunch. Well actually, the dog was sitting on the floor, but he looked at me the same way they did. No one asked me where I'd been or how I was—they just looked at me. They looked at me with a look I had come to recognize from my family when they didn't know what to do—they just looked at me. Naturally that Saturday night I drank, and then Sunday I drank again. My husband was supposed to leave town on a business trip Sunday, but he was afraid to leave me with the children, so he changed his plans and went to his office in Valley Forge. By the time he came home Monday evening I had once more begun drinking.

I had a few drinks and went into the kitchen to get another—it was early evening—and I found out there was no alcohol in the house! Now you understand I had always maintained an adequate supply in the house (some non-alcoholics might say more than adequate)—I might run out of ketchup but I wouldn't run out of Scotch—so I knew my husband must have poured it down the sink. I went into a rage—I was really out of my mind at the thought I couldn't get a drink *in my own house.*

I called my husband horrible names and I took down two large carving knives off the kitchen knife rack and I went after him threatening to kill him—at the very least I wanted to hurt him a lot. He was a lot bigger than I was and he just flipped the knives out of my hands, and he laughed at me—which made me even more furious. I told him that when he went to bed, he better not close his eyes. And it could be some outside power intervened in my life that night (some people would call it *God*) because I not only didn't kill my husband, I didn't put a mark on him—I passed out pretty much peacefully in the living room.

Now you know, it's a funny thing. For many years previous to that, at least ten, I had been a nightmare sleeper five or six nights a week. I had horrible dreams of rodents and reptiles and fences with spikes on them, and most nights I woke up screaming. This night however I didn't have a nightmare—I had what I now think of as my white dream. In the dream there was a large window with no curtains and glistering white sunlight poured in that window almost as white as diamonds. I had never had a dream like that before, and I just dismissed it—I didn't even mention it to my sponsor (when I got a sponsor) for five or six months. I was glad the horrible nightmares had gone—they've never come back—but I really didn't think much about the dream itself. But the day after the dream was a totally different day from the days that had gone before.

That morning—Tuesday—began differently from any day in a long time. I didn't drive to the liquor store; I didn't call the other liquor store that delivered to your home in an unmarked blue station wagon and even took a check; I didn't call my friend Kelly who lived four houses away and always had a good supply at her house. Instead I called the lady I had met the year before at the A.A. meeting. I asked her if they still had that meeting Tuesday night at the Episcopal Church there in Moorestown, and when she said they did, I told her I'd be there. I learned later she didn't think I would make it. But I did. By that first night after I had swallowed my last drink, I was at a meeting, had a sponsor, and had begun to try sobriety. We'll get to that "sponsor" business again a little later on.

Back then, in 1969 and 1970, I was told alcoholism was a disease and that it was incurable, progressive, and fatal—that if I continued drinking the way I'd been drinking, I was likely to wind up in jail, or in a mental institution, or being dead. To put it more exactly, I was told, as I said in the beginning, that alcoholism was a primary chronic disease that was often progressive and fatal—characterized by continuous or periodic impaired control over drinking, preoccupation with alcohol, use of alcohol despite adverse consequences, and distortions in thinking, most notably denial. And that its end was in jails, institutions, or death—or sobriety. I had already been in institutions (that's plural), and I figured the next stage would be jail or death, neither of which I really wanted. And when I went to meetings and heard the stories, I began to realize that death or jail were far closer than I had pretended.

It happened that when I had been sober a few months, I was asked to go with an older woman into the Camden County Jail (New Jersey), Women's Section. It happened this way: A woman named Kathy called me—her car wasn't running and she had worked out an arrangement with another woman to pick her up, but the other woman's car wouldn't work either and she needed me to take her to the jail, to take a meeting in to the women inmates.

I told her *No*—I didn't know anything about jails and I wouldn't be of any use, and Kathy just said, well, I'll have to mention this to Kay—so I went. Kathy told me to bring a box of Kleenex throwaway tissues (for blotting people's tears), a carton of cigarettes (this was a long time ago), and a Big Book. When I picked her up I had the supplies. We drove down to Camden and parked and we took our stuff in. They patted us down and they may even have taken our jewelry—in fact I think they did. And a matron said to follow her to the other side of the cell block—that is, through to the other side of the men's cell block, going right through the men's section of the jail—and I was terrified.

We got to the other end of the men's cell-block and there was a door that opened into a large room on the left with beds, a shower, two sinks, a toilet, and nine or ten female inmates sitting at two cedar picnic tables. They were waiting for us (actually they were mostly waiting for the cigarettes), and we all read the Big Book. The Kleenex tissues were barely touched, but just about everyone there was chain-smoking the cigarettes we had brought in. After reading we talked about some of the problems we'd had with drinking, Kathy and I, but no one identified with them.

They blamed their being in jail on a bum cop, a lousy john, a rotten husband or boy friend—everything happened *to* them. When we were leaving the matron pointed us to the other side of the room which had the female juveniles, who were kept in an area behind something that looked like large heavy chicken-wire. There were bunk beds, and girls about fourteen years old—one of them was pregnant. I had a hard time in that section—I had two stepdaughters and seeing these young girls there really hurt. As we left they put their little hands or fingers out through the wire to touch us. We went back out through the men's cell block and got our jewelry and money back, and we were glad to get out. I can still see those little fingers reaching through the wire, although the fourteen-year-olds who were there that day must be nearly fifty now, if they're still alive.

We were allowed to go back every other Tuesday, and we learned that although the male inmates had been receiving meetings for years, Kathy and I were the first to take a meeting in for the Camden County women. When Kathy called me that morning, I certainly didn't think going to a prison commitment would make any real difference in my life. I would have bet against it, and if I'd been telling you my story then, over thirty years ago, it would have been only a diversion in what I thought was the main story. And if I'd been telling it twenty years ago, it wouldn't have been nearly as important a part of my story as it is now.

But our stories change over time, as we change. Even though what happened in 1971 still happened in 1971, it's different when seen from 2005 or 2006. I went to other prisons after that, with other people, and twenty years later, when my husband died, I went to our local Community College, and when I had signed up, I talked to a very nice lady who showed me a list of possible courses of study. I looked down that list and there was Criminal Justice. I told her what I had selected (I was a 51-year old widow), and she suggested Art History instead. I took my Criminal Justice courses anyway, and did well enough that I got into an Honors program. In fact as part of that program, I eventually took Honors Art History—and it was one of the best courses I've ever taken, so she was right in a way—but she hadn't seen those young fingers reaching out to me through the cage.

When I finished community college (with my Criminal Justice concentration) I was working part-time for a temp agency until I could find full-time employment. One day I got a phone call from the temp agency asking if I would be willing to work behind the walls at Camp Hill Prison. The lady at the temp agency didn't know about the A.A. meetings I had led at the Camden County jail, but when I said I was certainly willing to work in a penal institution, she made an appointment for me at Camp Hill Prison, and in a couple of weeks I was working for one of the leaders in corrections in the state of Pennsylvania. One of my jobs was preparing pre-parole documents, including the inmates' records and their problems, including problems with alcohol and drugs. And you know, a lot of the time, if you talked to them, they were like the women in the county jail who believed that everything happened *to* them. Somehow they hadn't done *anything* themselves.

I learned a huge amount there and thereafter about drug and alcohol treatment in the corrections field, and not all of it matched my own knowledge of how things had to be done in order to work successfully— for example, releasing an inmate with a stipulation he get to just one or two A.A. meetings a week. After working at Camp Hill for a while, I was transferred to the Training Academy, setting up training courses for Corrections Officers. I have never thought enough attention was given to training prison workers how to work with alcoholics. After all, prisons and jails make up the largest group of rehabilitation facilities in this country.

One of my first reactions to the Camden County Jail back in 1970-71 was being happy that, when we finished our meeting, the door closed and locked with Kathy and me on the right side of it. You might say, that was a true feeling, and it has remained with me. But that was only the very beginning. If you go into A.A., you'll find that not all service opportunities have or will have the shattering and life-revising effect that Camden County Jail had on me—and thirty-five years later, I'm not sure this part of my story has stopped developing yet. I can see more clearly now, partly because I can think more clearly now, because my mind has learned new ways of thinking—in fact, my brain has learned new patterns of neural transmission—through year by year of sobriety.

When I was young, long before A.A., even before I took my first drink, we used to play a game called "Whisper Down the Lane"—I've heard people in other places called it "Telephone"—where you would whisper something to the person next to you, and they would whisper it to the person next to them, and so on down the line, until it got to the person who started it, and then everyone would laugh at how the message got all messed up. But this is "Whisper Down the Lane" in reverse. Every time I hear myself tell my story; every time I hear you tell your story; every time I hear a speaker or read a story in the back of the Big Book or even listen to a tape; I hear it better and better, and I see the true pattern better and better. We've already talked about this when we were discussing telling my story (or yours) in the previous section of the book.

In between (and during) service work of various kinds, I listened. I was told that the disease could be arrested by not drinking ever, and the best way to do that, by most estimations, was Alcoholics Anonymous. Now I didn't ask, *What's a disease?* I figured I could come up with an answer to that if I had to—I mean, we all know what a disease is—right? (It turns out, as I discovered, it isn't that simple, which is part of this section of this book.) I didn't ask, *Does A.A. work?* I was told, if you don't like A.A., you can leave, we'll gladly refund your misery. They didn't try to sell A.A.—I don't think I would have been buying. The closest they came to "selling" was saying, *This is what worked for us.* And if you don't want it, you can go away. What worked for them, I was told, was the Twelve Steps of Alcoholics Anonymous. How did I learn to practice the Twelve Steps? I guess the answer is, for me, I learned them by doing them, even when I didn't know I was doing them.

The night I asked Kay to be my sponsor, she told me, first, not to drink under any circumstances, second to call her frequently and at the sign of any confused thinking, third to get the phone numbers of experienced women like Mary K. and Pat C. who had been sober a while, fourth to go to as many meetings as I could and at least one meeting a week that was a step meeting, for as long as I was in the program, and finally she told me not to give my phone number to men. I asked her why she said that about giving my phone number to them, and she said *because I said so.* I asked her again and said I didn't know what that had to do with not drinking, and I don't remember if she ever did say anything except *don't do it.*

But what Kay told me began me on the first steps. I called her one time when I was having difficulty, and one of the things I asked her about was resentments—I didn't know what a resentment was. That was about a week after I had called her and said I wasn't speaking to my husband. She told me now that this was a resentment. After a little while—not long— she told me it was give-back time, and I needed a job in the group. We had coffee urns on all the tables and doughnuts at every meeting—someone could come in very new who had not eaten all day—sugar bowls and cream pitchers with tops, and china cups and saucers. The other thing was, I was sent around to other groups to speak—sometimes it was a two-speaker meeting and I was one of them, but sometimes there was only one speaker, and I was it!

I would have said Kay didn't give me much on the steps, but when I think about it, she was at the step meeting, and they had a break—a lot of the meetings did—where we could discuss what had been said. I also drove her to and from meetings, and we talked a lot in the car. We talked about God a lot, because I had a serious objection to God. I also had a period of seriously wanting a drink, badly. She told me I needed a relationship with a Higher Power, or I would drink. She was very insistent on that. I was convinced she was right, but I still wasn't convinced about God, and I didn't see how I could have a relationship with Someone or Something I didn't believe in. She gave me a white card, and told me to pray that prayer on the card—it was the Serenity Prayer—but I marked out "God" with a black marker. Even doing that though, and beginning the prayer without the word *God*—"Grant me the serenity"—it still worked. At least, I stayed in A.A., I did the steps, and I'm still sober thirty-five years later.

In a way—a very good way for me—those talks with Kay, in the "breaks" and in the car and even (though not so much) on the phone, and my listening at the step meeting, were my first three steps. I knew my life was unmanageable and I knew I didn't have control over my drinking— but every time I talked to Kay, I had to admit it, and not only that, by the fact I was talking to Kay, I was part of a "we" that were admitting it, particularly when she talked to me about her experience, which went back to 1951 in A.A. and before that in the New York drinking circles that produced many of the early A.A. members in that city.

Her long conversations with me about God, and her offer to believe while I prayed without belief, were part of my coming to believe that a "power greater than myself" could get me back on the track. And I did make the decision—actually we made the decision for me—to turn my life and my will over, just as she had and the other members of the group had. This first group where I was a member may have been the oldest group in that area. My sponsor was sober nineteen years in 1970, and I understand she didn't get sober the first time she came to A.A., so she had been around longer than the nineteen years. Some of the other members were sober a longer time, and one of them was Frank R.

Frank was well up in years and owned a retail establishment in town, and he knew everyone—everyone in our groups and everyone in surrounding groups. I remember when I first came to A.A., I was in the habit of arriving late during the preamble that opened the meeting, and leaving early during the Lord's Prayer that closed the meeting, and I tried very hard not to participate in the meeting in between. I was twenty-nine years old and the youngest person and one of the only females around, and I really thought one of these nights Frank was going to come along and pat me on the head and say "That's all right, Janie, you don't need to come anymore." Instead of that he came to me one night and said to me, "Sweetie, the time has come to be on time." I was mortified, but I wasn't late again—that's not to say I've *never* been late, but the times have been few and far between and when I'm hurrying to make a meeting, I still hear Frank's voice saying, "Sweetie, the time has come to be on time."

These old-timers really didn't miss much: I can remember lingering in the parking lot after a meeting talking to a man, and someone coming up to me and saying, "Isn't it time for you to get home?" I was wild, and I thought, who are they to be saying that?—but after that I never lingered in a parking lot after a meeting talking to a man. There was another old-timer a little later—actually Rita wasn't really an old timer but she had that aura—she came up to me after a meeting—she was a little gal with tiny fingers and I can still see her little finger poking at my chest when she said, "You, my dear, are not getting to enough meetings!" I was so wild I didn't go to that meeting for a while and I didn't speak to Rita or her husband even if I saw them at other meetings or around—I had a terrible resentment though I didn't know that's what it was—she wasn't even my sponsor and she spoke to me like *that*!

After about a month I had to say something about it to someone. It was festering inside me. My brother picked me up for a meeting and I told him about it and asked him what he thought. He said Rita was right—this from my own brother—and I thought the God I was now believing in had turned on me. He not only said Rita was right, he said that the minute it happened I should have spoken to someone about it. I said sarcastically, "Well, who exactly do you think I should have talked to about it?" and he said, "Anyone, sister—it didn't matter just so long as you got rid of that burden." It took me quite a while to get over all this—what Rita said and what my brother said—but I did, and in the end I got to see that Rita was right—I wasn't getting to enough meetings. I stepped up my meeting attendance and finally I was able to say to Rita, "You remember that night when you said I wasn't getting to enough meetings—you were right."

When I was sober five or six years, I developed thyroid cancer—I was treated twice with liquid radiation and I was afraid and my family was very afraid—my mother especially. I was having some trouble with dizziness and brief faints at a time I was very active in A.A., on the steering committee of a large city intergroup, and I went to my doctor for a checkup and told him I was worried about driving my car, and should I cut back on my activities—since I had this medical problem maybe I was into too much and maybe I should drop some things. He said to me "Miss S____, don't you drop anything, you stay as close to this A.A. as you can—if you need transportation and you're worried about driving, get someone to take you. I have enough patients sitting around in rocking chairs who don't have what you have and you should stick to it." He was right. When I was pregnant a couple of years later, there was concern about the radiation, but I was as fine as could be and so was the baby. You know, I find that sometimes there's a tendency to retreat to fear when if only we hang tight together, we'll make it through.

PART TWO

DOING INVENTORY AND
MAKING AMENDS

Kay H. died while I working on my Fourth Step. Actually, I had pretty much completed it, but I hadn't done my Fifth, when Kay died. I was just congratulating myself that no one would know I hadn't done the Fifth, or at least I could put it off for a while, when Mary K. told me I was going to be at her house on Saturday morning, between 8:00 and 8:30, to do my Fifth. Sometime around 1 p.m. we were through. There was a sense of validation coming from revealing myself to someone so much like myself, to another alcoholic, in a way that was not restricted by the restraints of talking to a clergyman or professional psychiatrist. I realized then, and have realized many times since, the value of taking that Fifth Step. For me, it began to open me up so that the fellowship could work with me and through me.

Now as soon as I finished Step Five, Mary told me to review what I had done. She told me to thank God—I still wasn't completely sure about this God and about believing in Him (or "It," I thought)—for what He had given me. She told me to review the first five steps to be certain I had followed them as carefully as I could. I was told this Sixth Step Review would be reassuring for the alcoholic who has done the steps well enough (me, I hoped), and a reminder to do better to the alcoholic who hasn't. I thought I was in the first category, though I wasn't entirely sure. But when I thought of sitting there in Mary's kitchen those hours, and how different it had been from the counseling and psychiatry, I was pretty sure. So—on to Step Seven!

I thought, at that time, that for me Step Seven was the easiest of the Twelve, and in many ways it was. That was also the beginning of my really learning about my Higher Power (I had been one of those who started off considering the group as my higher power). You see, I knew by the time I got through the Sixth Step Review that it pretty much had to have been a

Higher Power who had relieved me of the need to drink and I believed (at least I think I believed) that this Higher Power could relieve me of anger, sloth, lust—and also pride, gluttony, greed, envy—I was pretty traditional in my list of character defects. They were the Seven Deadly Sins of my mother's Catholic upbringing. I had been to counseling—individual private counseling and group counseling—and I had read a lot of books about the flaws in my personality, and I believed I was as powerless over them as I was over alcohol. But you know, it isn't really that easy. Here's another place where my story changed along the way.

You might say my *expanded* Seventh Step was done with a later sponsor, in Pennsylvania, whom I call "Big Book Mary." She was the one who told me not to expect that my praying meant that these problems would be immediately amended. They may be, but that's not for me to decide. I don't decide when and how I'm to be relieved of sloth and anger and lust. I don't get up in the morning and say "Today I'm not going to be slothful or angry or lustful." You might say that these defects are "under another jurisdiction." And that other jurisdiction doesn't work on my time.

This was frustrating to me—it still is—but at least I know that greater and greater release from the power of my character defects will happen if I do my part. The point is, I have a part. It has seemed to me that I just go along and go along, and after some time has gone by, I'm not as slothful as before, and then after more time has gone by, I can see even more improvement in that area, and that's how it works. If I keep asking and keep remembering about sloth, I will be conscious of it when I'm slothful. If I keep asking and keep remembering about envy, I will be conscious of it when I'm being envious. If I keep asking and keep remembering about lust, I will be conscious of it when I'm lustful. If I keep asking and keep remembering about anger, I will be conscious of it when I'm angry. And so on for each one of those behavior patterns that are called the Seven Deadly Sins.

Some people, when they're telling their stories, combine the Eighth and Ninth steps in telling about any particular person on their list, going right into what they did, but I'm keeping the two separate. First the list of the people to whom I'm going to make amends, along with the slowly developing willingness to make the amends—all of them!—and then the Ninth

Step, where I make the amends. I started my Eighth Step in New Jersey under the guidance of Jane S. (that's another Jane S., of course) and Mary K. in South Jersey. The list of those I had harmed included people in addition to the ones I had harmed in the years I was drinking. On the top of the list of those I had harmed were my mother and my husband (and I'm not sure of the order I put them in). I knew I had hurt my mother in my teens, when I began drinking, but also before my teens (before I began drinking).

I had a record of attempting suicide. I began sessions with a psychiatrist when I was fifteen or sixteen, when I first began to disappear, and by my early twenties I was disappearing for longer times and longer distances from my home. Naturally my mother spent a great deal of her time in worry, and of course I never thought of anyone in this connection except myself. There was the time I ran over my brother with his car (he wasn't hurt, so I couldn't understand what the big hoopla was).

My husband (he was my second husband) I loved more than anyone else in the world (I believed) but when I drank I threw it all out the window. I didn't care about his concern, his nights of worry when I would disappear, and his additional worry when I was driving drunk—not to mention his concern as to whether he could go off on a trip and safely leave his daughters with me. And I loved them too—still do—I talked to my younger step-daughter yesterday and the day before.

Next on my list was my brother, two years younger than I. We fought a great deal, and about ninety percent of the fights were my choice—I forced them—because my brother didn't like to fight that way. I embarrassed him in front of his friends, sometimes with the language I used, and sometimes, in a bar with a good band playing, because I didn't always remain entirely clothed, and certainly did not remain in my right mind.

And along with my brother, there were my two stepdaughters, nine years apart, four and thirteen, and the thirteen-year-old was humiliated by my rudeness and my yelling at her in front of her friends. I even hit her one time. The younger one was four: I knew I owed her amends simply because … simply because … because I owed her amends for things I couldn't specify at that time, but I knew they were there. I have since been able to specify them and I have identified and listed them. As I say, a recovering alcoholic's story changes over time—that's part of the combined narrative of drinking and sobriety. The story changes in the telling because of the telling, and it gets closer to the ultimate truth, not further away.

I had a couple of friends to whom I knew I had to make amends. I had an aunt who I thought was harsh on just about everyone, and I was rude to her and critical of the way she treated my cousins and me. The uncle I knew I needed to make amends to, was really very supportive and helpful and kind to me, but somehow I misread his attempts to be supportive and helpful and kind. You understand, I have quite a number of uncles and aunts and cousins, and they all had their places on the list of people I had not treated well, but what I'm talking about now is the people way up on the list of those to whom I had really done the greatest harm, the people I had really hurt the most.

There was my first husband and his parents, and Millie. Millie was a 1958 Fiat automobile, blue with gray trim, clutch, and no radio, and she was lent to me by my ex-father-in-law, my first husband's father, when I was discharged—again!—from the local state mental hospital in the fall of 1965. I didn't have a car and I didn't have money to buy one and I needed a place to live and a job and a car to get there. My former mother-in-law and father-in-law, who both drove big four-door Jaguars, lent me their spare car, Millie. In those days if you drove a Jaguar, let alone two of them, you *needed* a spare car! In the 50s and 60s, Jaguars were such finely tuned and highly powered racing autombiles that they could get out of whack easily, but as I remember it, Jaguar owners were invariably proud of how much time their cars spent in the repair shop.

I was more than grateful for their loan, and I took very good care of Millie, including putting on the emergency brake every time I parked, so she wouldn't roll down hill. Unfortunately I was a drinker who drank everywhere and anywhere—my place or yours or the nearest saloon. Since I didn't have a place of my own then and was living with my aunt (the state hospital wouldn't discharge me to live at my mother's but I was given a limited discharge to live at my aunt's), I pretty much drank in saloons. One night I went to several saloons and I didn't really know my way around (this wasn't near where I'd lived before), and the next morning Millie was gone—really gone. I didn't even know whether I had left Millie in Pennsylvania or New Jersey. I called everywhere, and had someone drive me around, and there were no 1958 blue Fiats with gray trim and a clutch and no radio. Moment by moment my heart beat faster and I had to admit—to myself at first—that I had no idea where the car was, and the more I looked the less I knew. I called Dad—my first father-in-law was always Dad to me as long as he lived—and I told him I didn't know where Millie was. He and my ex-husband and some of their friends came to where I was living and undertook a search and they were positive they were going to find the car but no such luck—no Millie anywhere, ever.

Of course I apologized many times over—I cried—I couldn't sleep—but the fact remained, I had borrowed the car and lost it. Everyone was as kind to me and as understanding as they could be. They knew I had serious problems, and no one gave me a hard time for a moment—except me. You know sometimes we're hardest on ourselves, and this was the case with me and Millie. When I finally got sober, both of my first husband's parents were dead, but they were on my amends list.

I wrote a brief letter, apologizing, saying that I was truly sorry, that I was grateful to them for how kind they had been to me and I was sober now—my life was taking a new turn. Even though I knew that wouldn't replace Millie, even if they were still here, I prayed that this kind of behavior from me was gone forever. I had come to know that Millie would never have been lost if it hadn't been for me being a blackout drinker. Coming to know this made it possible for me to tell my story more truthfully, and to make a real—not a self-pitying—apology, though I couldn't restore Millie and I had to make my amends by prayer.

There was one person on my Eighth Step list that I didn't get in touch with to make amends. When I was drinking, I had an affair with her husband. Kay told me, when I talked it over with her, that I wouldn't be able to get relief by confessing to her and making amends. There's a place in the Ninth Step where it says we make direct amends "except when to do so [to make amends] would injure them [the persons we're making amends to] or others." (Whether I am included with "the others" who might be harmed isn't important right now, and there's some disagreement among the A.A. old timers on that.)

My amends were made first to those closest to me, who were the ones I felt I had harmed the most. First was my husband—the man who put up with my drinking, my disappearing act, my blowing money away, my verbal abuse—the man who almost literally dragged me to those first six A.A. meetings, where I could not or would not identify as an alcoholic. I told him that I was deeply sorry for what I had done and that I hoped and believed that as long as I was following this way of life I would never do these things again. That was the beginning of my amends. My living the way I should have been all along was the next part.

The marriage didn't work out with me sober, and we were divorced, and my stepdaughters went back to their mother, but I'm still in touch with my second husband. Before our break-up, he helped me a lot, going to open meetings with. me, listening to speakers, and stoking up at potluck suppers. And you know, after we broke up, he has still kept in touch—he came to the hospital when my son was born—and it's not long ago that he gave my son some good stereo components. They've always been on good terms, which was more than can be said of my son's father. Indeed, when my son was born, it was my former husband who brought my mother to see us in the hospital (and of course came with her).

The second person I made amends to was my older stepdaughter, who was thirteen at the time. She had suffered (as only a twelve- and thirteen-year-old can) from my nasty disposition, rotten language, and (I'm sorry to say) an occasional slap including one in front of her best friend—she also suffered from the knowledge that I had gone out with someone other than her father, in our first year of marriage. She was so thrilled that I stopped drinking that when she was assigned to write a school report about a medical problem, she wrote on alcoholism including a poster and a talk in front of her class in which she said her stepmother was an alcoholic and didn't drink anymore and she was really glad—so much for Alcoholics *Anonymous* but I was really touched. She's married, three children (no grandchildren yet) and lives in Florida, and we're still distantly in touch.

Next on the amends list was my younger stepdaughter who was four. She didn't know what this was all about, but she said she thought it was great (I guess she had the word from her older sister). I took her up into my lap and started to talk to her, and then I started to cry. She asked me why I was crying and I told her, and I said, "Sometimes I cry when I'm losing my mind." It wasn't something I chose to say—it just came out. She looked at me and said, "Mommy, I always cry when I'm losing my mind." She knew I needed to be comforted—needed to know we were together, despite all I had said and done—and we were. The relationship that comes out of the amends can be part of the continuing process of the amends, as it was (and is) here.

The next was my mother, who flat out refused to speak to me. My brother likewise. I remember being really heartbroken and saying to my sponsor, "What's the use? I'm trying to do the right thing and the people I love the most won't even let me in." (That's self-pity.) She told me that when we make the amends, all we take care of is making the amends to those on the list—what happens then isn't up to us. She told me I had to keep praying for my mother and brother, and pray until the hurt stopped hurting. It never stopped hurting, but I went on praying—the Serenity Prayer and the prayer in the story in the back of the Big Book called "Freedom from Bondage" (on page 552)—never knowing what would happen and not trying to predict or outline. I couldn't have predicted what did happen.

A year and a half into my sobriety (it was February 1972) the phone rang one Thursday night. It was my brother and he wanted to know if I was still staying off the sauce. I told him I was. He said, "Nothing at all?" I told him, not a drop! He asked me to tell him what to do. I picked him up the next night for a meeting, and gave him a Big Book. He died twenty-three years later, sober, never having had a drink from that night. Not sure why it happened that way, but it did.

I was sober almost four years—it was a Sunday evening—when my mother called. I was overwhelmed at hearing from her after such a long time. She was crying and then so was I, and she said she had just had what she hoped was her last drink—the glass was on the counter in the kitchen and she hoped never to have a drink again. I don't know what brought her to this point, but the next night my brother and I took her to a meeting. She never had another drink and died sober thirteen years later. Our little family was getting together again, and while it wasn't perfect, it was better than before. I believe my mother and brother would not have gotten in touch with me without my attempts to make amends—and whether that's true or not, I know the meetings and the new relationship with them were part of my amends.

I had a number of what I think of as more "routine" amends to people I mentioned before, when I was talking about the Eighth Step—I've mentioned my first husband, his parents, my best friend, another friend, my aunt, my uncle, a cousin. All of those other amends were what I could call successful—they were kind to me, receptive, and I got out from under a lot of the burden of the past. In fact, except for my mother and brother—and you see how well that eventually turned out—no one I went to, to make my amends, gave any appearance of being critical. I don't know what would have happened to me if I hadn't learned about this amends process, with its opportunities for new self-examination and getting out from under the burden of remorse. Other people may be able to stay sober without making amends—I'm pretty sure I wouldn't have.

And then came Step Ten. Over the years it's been really hard for me to put down my true experience with Step Ten because I never liked it, and I told myself it was a duplication of what I did in Step Four, and I wanted to get on with it, not keep going back. It took me till after I had done Eleven and Twelve to see the real value of Step Ten. The part of Step Ten I've done best with, is the use of the "spot check inventory"—I can go along in the course of a day, and everything seems fine and I feel great and all's well with the world—and then somehow I begin to feel a little bit uncomfortable—maybe a little bit queasy. There's an old saying that your head can lie to you six days out of seven, but your gut never will lie to you.

So I get this uneasy feeling and I know something is wrong—something I've said, something I've done, some attitude that has crept in. For example, I've been known to be sarcastic and think nothing of it, but *others* don't "think nothing of it," and I need to make a spot check inventory on my sarcasm and do something about it, and do something about the damage it's done. If my grandson is getting on my nerves (he's ten and *very* energetic) and I speak to him too harshly, when I see the look on his face, that starts a spot check inventory. And I can tell you, for me and for every alcoholic I've ever sponsored, we need to know how our harsh words can hurt, and that hurt can go on and on if we don't make our spot check and do something about the hurting we have caused. After thirty five years, I don't do as well as I should, but I do a lot better than I used to.

It is recommended in the Big Book that we watch out for selfishness, dishonesty, resentment, and fear. "When these crop up we ask God to remove them." I have found that the more quickly I can make an amend to someone, the better I feel—I think the better they feel too, but I know the better I feel. "Love and tolerance of others is our code." The thought of Jane S. being loving and tolerant of others is something I have to keep always in my mind. I strive for love and tolerance, I hope for love and tolerance, and I pray for love and tolerance. It can be very easy for me to rest and lie back, because I'm sober, and I've been sober for a while, and I'm active in the program, and I try to help other alcoholics—so sometimes I get to think that I'm the one calling the shots. As my son used to say, "Not!"

Sometimes I forget there's something or someone (or Something or Someone) behind every move I make. When I can keep that thought in the forefront of my thinking, I do much better with everyone in my life—family, co-workers, others in A.A. Keeping that thought where it belongs—always present in my mind—comes out of my taking inventory. And another thing—I keep a watch for those who are going smoothly through life and I try to emulate them—I have heard it said they become living copies of the Big Book for this alcoholic. But I won't know how the emulation is doing if I don't take inventory. Also, some A.A. members make a major inventory review an annual or every-six-months event. I don't know whether that comes under the Fourth Step or the Tenth Step (some say it's an annual Fourth Step, some say it's part of a continuing Tenth) but it's a great idea—we can't keep too well informed about the way we are and the way we are coming across to others.

PART THREE

PRAYER, MEDITATION, AND TWELFTH STEP WORK

When I came to A.A. the mere thought of even praying was beyond anything I could entertain, but you know, as I slowly absorbed the wisdom of the fellowship, by the time I got to Step Eleven, it was no longer something I couldn't imagine doing—I had started to pray and gradually it had become comfortable and something I could do on a regular basis. The first prayer I became familiar with was the Lord's Prayer (the "Our Father") that we said then (and mostly say now) at the end of every meeting. I had known the Lord's Prayer as a school girl and could say it almost automatically. The second prayer I was given was the Serenity Prayer, where I was a little uncomfortable, because I didn't know the prayer. But the discomfort passed away and I have used the Serenity Prayer for years—"God, grant me the serenity to accept the things I cannot change, courage to change the things I can, and wisdom to know the difference." My first serious use of the Serenity Prayer was when I was afflicted with a desire to drink—I didn't really want to drink, and I knew if I gave in I'd lose everything including my family—yet the desire to drink was still there, and one day when it was particularly strong my sponsor gave me the little white card with the Serenity Prayer. She told me I didn't have to believe, I just had to pray it—she believed and the rest of the group believed and that was enough. So I went home and prayed the Serenity Prayer, and don't you know, I didn't pick up a drink that day in late 1970, and I still haven't, and I think there's a connection. My sponsor told me I had to have a relationship with God or I would never be sober. I've been working on that relationship ever since then and I've never regretted it.

The meditation, however, came with much more difficulty than the prayer. I would sit down, put my feet on the floor, my hands in my lap, and try to close my mind to the outside world. It never worked, though for several years I tried and tried. My mind would never stop racing. It went on at a tremendous rate and I began to think that I was a hopeless case. I was embarrassed about this, and I had difficulty discussing it at meetings, and I wanted to be able to do it so badly. It was sometime after my first sponsor died and I came to Pennsylvania, when I told "Big Book Mary," my sponsor then, that I had done everything in the Steps so far but I just couldn't meditate. She said, "I think you can—let's try practicing it together." So I went over to her house and we sat down and we read from the Big Book and then I could sense her mind became quiet, and after a minute or two so did mine. I learned that for me it's much easier to practice the art of meditation in the company of another person or several other people, than it is to do it alone. And I had learned that it isn't by trying to close my mind off, but by letting it be opened up, that I could begin meditation.

I became aware there was a Step Twelve almost from the very time I came into A.A. I heard people talk about it at meetings, I heard speakers talk about their experience with Twelfth Step work and Twelfth Step calls—and I learned that my calling for help to the local Intergroup and their calling me back, and Kay meeting me at a meeting, and everyone trying to explain the program to me—this was all Twelfth Step work and I was the one who was being "Twelfth-Stepped." Like just about every other alcoholic I have ever met, my first experience of the Twelfth Step was on the receiving end—the giving came later, as it has to. You can't give away what you don't have.

Now when I was sober about four months, I was in a real slump—my thinking was really low, it got harder and harder to get myself to a meeting, and sometimes I even wanted to drink. My sponsor was a very experienced A.A. and she recognized the symptoms of real trouble, so she and the chairman of our group arranged a job—a "service position"—for me. I've told you about that earlier, but it goes with this part of my story too, because it's an example of Twelfth-Step work that I didn't recognize then, but I recognize now, so my story has changed because my way of thinking has changed. That's important.

I was out in the kitchen washing dishes after a meeting, and when I came out of the kitchen, my sponsor and the chairman said they had a job for me. I thought they were wrong—there wasn't any job for me but wash-ing dishes—I was sober such a short time and had such a dim view of my capabilities that I couldn't imagine anyone would want me to do a job. But they had it all mapped out—I was to be the "Librarian" and get the name and date of last drink of each member of the group—and their phone numbers if I wanted them—and put it down in this ledger. And the week before our business meeting, which was the last Tuesday of the month, I was to call the chairman and give the name and year number of the anniversaries that month, so it could be put on the anniversary cake at the last meeting of the month. It was a big event—remember, there weren't any chips and medallions for sobriety time back then.

It took a while for me to figure out why I was made the group librar-ian—though it should have been pretty obvious. But you know, when you're only sober a short time, you don't do very well looking at yourself. I was very shy. I had trouble talking to people. I never said *hello*. I never called anyone on the phone. I never asked for help. I never offered help. And here I was with the responsibility of walking up to every member of that group and asking them their name and date of last drink. The job was tailor-made for me. The greatest scaredy cat in the county was talking to everyone. You know, I'll never forget that whole experience and the people who dreamed it up. Being group librarian may have saved my sobriety—I don't know—but it certainly got me to interact on a social plane with other alcoholics.

A lot of the jobs in A.A. do that—get us on a plane with other alco-holics and get us thinking of others—which my experience tells me isn't a natural state for an alcoholic. My second experience with Step Twelve sup-posedly had me on the giving end, but I was still receiving. I've told you about Kathy R. dragging me to the Camden County Jail with an A.A. meeting for female inmates. This was another example of my being hurled out of my very small world into a much bigger place—where I needed to be—and a place that needed me and still needs members of this fellow-ship—prisons—one of the triple threat of jails, institutions, and death that lie in wait for alcoholics who go back to drinking.

It says in the Big Book in Chapter Seven that "practical experience shows that nothing will so much insure immunity from drinking as intensive work with other alcoholics. It works when other activities fail." This has been true in my case and probably for everyone I know. When we reach out for the other alcoholic, when we crawl out of our own world for the other alcoholic, my experience is that what we get back is beyond measure.

The step mentions that we try to practice these principles in all our affairs. Sometimes this is really tough. When someone at home or on the job (or that kook who lives next door) tries our patience, it can really be tough to hold on to principles of love and service and not be judgmental or critical. In fact, talking about "that kook who lives next door" is judgmental all by itself, so we're much better off saying "my next-door neighbor"—even if she is a kook! These principles pay off in all of our affairs with all of the people in our lives, and whenever we can be kind and generous with others, it works. And one other thing—if we have another problem besides alcoholism—like tobacco—we can use the same set of procedures and principles.

The Step says, "Having had a spiritual awakening as the result of these steps, we tried to carry this message to alcoholics, and to practice these principles in all our affairs." That's three parts—spiritual awakening, carrying the message, practicing the principles in all our affairs.

About this spiritual awakening. By the time I first got to Step Twelve at the Tuesday night Step Meeting—I had gone through the first eleven—a lot had happened in my life that was different from anything that had happened before. First of all, I hadn't had a drink and I wasn't planning on getting one. Secondly, I wasn't running roughshod over the emotions of the people in my world. I wasn't stepping on people the way I had for so many years. I was sharing what had been given to me. But I hadn't yet *done* all the Steps leading up to Twelve.

Still, to the extent I could, I was sharing my time, my thoughts, my energy, to help others. And for the first time since I was a little girl, I had thoughts about God—I was beginning to have prayers I could say, I read about God, I went to meetings and heard people talk about how their lives had been affected by a Higher Power. I had never thought much—if at all—about caring for others, even though I was on my second marriage. I was still pretty much concerned about my own feelings. When I got to A.A., I just wanted to stop feeling the way I felt, stop hurting the way I hurt—which, when you think about it, is pretty selfish—but I found myself being turned in another direction now. I didn't even know I needed that turn, but (looking back on it) God knew, my sponsor knew, the members of my group knew. Looking back, it was really obvious that I was a loser. You know, Dr. Bob, one of A.A.'s co-founders, called his prospects pigeons because they came home to roost. I was Kay's pigeon and I'm glad she and the Moorestown Group were taking care of the nest when I came "home" to A.A.

You know, I can talk about *doing* the Steps, and say they're in order for a reason—and that's true, and we all talk that way—but my ability to give what I've been given increases as I have been given more and more, as I've been in the fellowship of Alcoholics Anonymous longer and longer, and as the quality of my Step work has gotten better—which means, I've been able to carry out my Twelfth-Step work better now that I've finished the first nine, and gotten better at the Tenth and Eleventh. Quite a number of the examples of the particular kind of Twelfth-Step work I've done in my sobriety have been of the kind called "service"—which usually means making sure meetings are held, groups continue to be active, publications are available, A.A. continues to be there for the next alcoholic to come in, and services like prison meetings and public information continue to be carried on. My third husband was great for getting meetings started up, and he was great at sponsorship. I've done both, including doing a lot of sponsoring, but a lot of what I've done was what you might say was a kind of office work for making sure A.A. continues to be here.

I was a group secretary at my first group in Pennsylvania, outside of Philadelphia—the group secretary is sometimes really the group chairman (it varies depending on the group)—but where I was group secretary, that just meant I took the minutes at all business meetings and transcribed them and presented them at the next business meeting. I was what is sometimes called a recording secretary. I've also been a Group Chairman (who is also sometimes called the Secretary in some groups, which is confusing for newcomers), and currently hold that position at my home Step and Tradition group—I chair the business meetings and select the weekly chairman, but I don't do minutes—now!

To be a group (recording) secretary sometimes requires six months to one year of sobriety, and the term is sometimes as short as six months (in rare cases shorter). To be a group chairman may require longer sobriety, and the term is usually one or two years. Sometimes being secretary requires a lot more serenity than usually comes after six months of sobriety. I can remember those business meetings when I was group secretary, which tended to be very large and very vocal. Everyone had a complaint about one thing or another and an axe (or a couple of axes) to grind about something else. For example, "So-and-so chaired last month and he got lousy speakers—can't we get better chairmen who get better speakers?" Or "Last month the coffee was too weak—*twice*!" Or "So-and-so forgot to get doughnuts last month—you can't have meetings without doughnuts!"

And then there was the business meeting where the complaint was, "The room was so crummy, it was hard to sit in it—couldn't somebody clean it?" In that case, a couple of somebodies ended up cleaning it, and even got permission from the landlord to paint it. Sometimes cups from the previous meeting were left in the sink unwashed—this was the most common complaint except for "The ashtrays weren't washed out thoroughly." (This was back when we had smoking meetings and china cups.)

These business meetings lasted close to an hour, and by the time they were over, everyone was exhausted—especially the secretary who had to take everything down. In fact, I wasn't quick enough to take everything down—especially when it got to the question of what was to be done about the addicts coming in from a local rehab and identifying as addicts, in our closed A.A. meeting (which meant alcoholics only). Having these rehab addicts coming into these closed A.A. meetings and identifying as addicts was more than some of the old timers could handle—they had come into the program under the sponsorship of still older old timers, who went back to before the Big Book was published in 1939.

It was such a serious problem that A.A.'s General Service Office in New York issued a white card that said, we speak about alcohol and alcoholism, and other things are mentioned "only in passing"—we read that at every meeting—I thought it was a good idea but the old timers thought it didn't go far enough and the addicts thought they didn't have enough space. The problem still hasn't been resolved in a lot of groups with a lot of people even now, thirty years later. The only thing that began to relieve the pressure back then was that people began to start Narcotics Anonymous (N.A.) meetings. But the problem was that those meetings mostly weren't as strong or organized, and didn't have people with as much sober time as at the A.A. meetings, so a lot of addicts continued to come to A.A. meetings because they needed the added strength.

Also, for a brief time, N.A. meetings in the Philadelphia area were the object of continuous police surveillance for drug activity. Once that stopped, attendance at N.A. meetings in the area increased. In the area where I now live there are good N.A. meetings, but back then, the addicts felt they needed A.A. meetings, and I guess some still do. But it can be—and to some degree it still is—a very real problem. It's hard for alcoholics to identify with drug addicts or pill poppers or overeaters, *even if* those drug addicts, pill poppers, etc., are *also* alcoholics. We have a Tradition (the Fifth Tradition) that speaks to our carrying the message to the *alcoholic* who still suffers.

We had our A.A. meetings five nights a week—they were all closed discussion meetings, except one was a closed step meeting. Our group had been founded by a man who got sober in Philadelphia at 4021 Walnut Street, who we thought was the greatest. He was a little guy, well up in years, physically a lightweight—but not a lightweight in A.A. He was a wonderful example of how to live sober, how to carry the message, and his own personal sobriety was extensive—when I came there he had been sober over thirty years.

We heard about an old hospital—it had been a tuberculosis hospital, I think—that was only a few miles away from where we held our meetings. We heard this hospital had been taken over as a "dually-addicted" rehab for people who had drug *and* alcohol problems. We heard about it in passing but didn't think much about it because, after all, *we* held meetings for alcoholics—we didn't even know any drug addicts (so far as we knew), and it never occurred to us that there would be any problem—or opportunity.

But one night—it was in the winter with a light, cold rain falling—in walked a man we had never seen, just when we were starting the meeting. He sat down, we had our speaker, we went to the discussion part of the meeting, and he introduced himself as an addict: "My name is ———— and I'm a drug addict." When he said that, he was sitting across the table from our founder Stan. Now the new man—he was in his early thirties—I'm sure he wasn't prepared for what happened when he said "and I'm a drug addict." Stan was up and out of his chair and across the table holding on to the new man's coat—I saw the new man's face and he looked terrified. Some of the guys on his side of the table got hold of the newcomer, some of the guys from the other side of the table got hold of Stan, and they tried to calm things down. We tried to tell our visitor this was a closed meeting for alcoholics, to which he said, "But I'm an addict and it's the same thing." And Stan got his breath and said, "Oh no it's not—if you want to come here, you better identify as an alcoholic!" I was sober only two years then, and I didn't know much about this, and I did know the guy was terrified, and I sensed he needed a meeting.

But, you know, he was told he could come back any time if he identified as an alcoholic—and he did that. But he went to other groups and identified as an addict, and the other groups didn't have a Stan, so he went on identifying himself there as an addict. The last I heard of him he wasn't sober—why I'm not completely sure, but for the several years I was in that area, he was in and out of A.A. several times, and he became a disruptive force at A.A. meetings, and I think maybe he had a problem with being different. I couldn't help wondering if being at the seat of so much controversy helped make his sobriety precarious. Of course my prayer is, that at some time since then, he's been able to accept the fact that the two illnesses are different (even if there are similarities), and that A.A. and N.A. are different.

The members of our group had a big party at a big country club with all sorts of wonderful food for Stan's thirty-third anniversary—and thirty male members and three female members (I was one of the three) were allotted one minute each to talk about Stan. (The country club party of course was *not* paid for out of group funds.) I was sober only a few years, and it was a highlight of my life to be asked to participate in something like this. It's a memory that's strongly with me now, thirty-plus years later, and I'm sure it will continue to be.

I've been treasurer of my home group once, when I lived outside of Philadelphia, in the 1970s, and treasurer of a local Intergroup Association (but not in or around Philadelphia). Treasurer has not been a service position I've particularly wanted—in my business life I've been Comptroller for at least two companies and done a decent job, but in A.A. I'd rather someone else handled the money. I think it's that I don't want my A.A. life to become routine so that I don't think about what I'm doing, or think that, "well, the numbers are small after being comptroller for X company, so it doesn't take as much vigilance."

When I was treasurer for my group, I don't recall much difficulty. The group was in a wealthy area—we had a lot of money—at times, at least. There were also times when we didn't. We paid all of our expenses. We spent money donating books—mostly Big Books—to schools, community libraries, and prisons. We bought the books from New York until the local Intergroup Association reduced its prices, and then we bought them locally. This whole business of distributing these books was what some people call a labor of love—we never knew how many people would read these books or even see them, but we knew our hearts were full, and we had a great desire to share wherever we could. We thought people who didn't know they were alcoholics might come across one of these books and look further into the matter to see if this applied to them or their family or friends. Whenever I hear someone say they first saw the Big Book in jail or in a school or a library, it gives me a warm feeling to know someone may have seen the books we distributed, and have gone on from there.

Another thing we did with our money, we had a good full literature rack, maybe two racks, and they were filled fat with literature—lots of copies of the standard A.A. brochures. We wanted anyone who saw the racks to know they weren't taking our last copy of anything. Another area where we spent money, was every year we sent our General Service

Representative (GSR) to the Poconos, for the weekend annual Area Convention/Assembly. What's a General Service Rep (GSR)?—we'll get to that—but we always had one. It was extremely important to us to have one. The last area where we spent money in that group, was we had an anniversary celebration with a speaker and a potluck supper every year. Everyone contributed.

I was told when I got into A.A, that maybe more than most people, alcoholics enjoy getting together with food. I really don't know *why* this is, but I do know *that* it is. Any gathering I've gone to where food is served has been a hit. The first time I was aware of this, my home group was having a potluck, with a movie on the Twelve Traditions which had been made by Bill W. The week we were preparing for that spread, I wanted to do something, so I asked my sponsor Kay, and she said, "My dear, alcoholics love chocolate and Italian." I made lasagna and there wasn't anything left of that, or much of anything else we had cooked. On the other hand, although I love Bill W. as much as anyone, I thought the movie was for the birds. Apparently I wasn't the only one who thought that way. We went on to have more potlucks—without the movie. Ever since then I've sometimes made lasagna or ziti or something else Italian, but mostly I've made chocolate cakes, and I've put them on the dessert table, and you know, chocolate goes before strawberry, peach, angel food cakes, or anything else. Alcoholics love chocolate and Italian! There's a group not far from where I am now that has an annual spaghetti dinner—it's standing room only, but if you can get in the door you'll get fed—spaghetti and meatballs, salad, garlic bread and a huge dessert table—and the chocolate goes first. Now when I make a chocolate cake for a meeting, my grandson says "I hope they don't eat it all!"—but a lot of time they do.

PART FOUR

DOING A.A. SERVICE WORK

When I was treasurer for the Intergroup Association, I was in no danger of failing to take it seriously, and also in no danger of falling into a routine. I better explain what an "Intergroup Association" is in A.A. It's a kind of central clearing-house for what's going on, usually in and around the largest city in a particular geographical area—like Philadelphia or Cleveland or New York. Each group in that city and the surrounding geographical area elects an Intergroup Representative, and these representatives elect a Steering Committee for the Intergroup, and this Steering Committee then sets up committees that carry out A.A. work such as distributing literature, and publishing meeting schedules, and taking meetings into prisons and institutions, and making the public and professional communities aware of A.A.

But on this business of being Intergroup Treasurer—this was eight or ten years ago, here in south-central Pennsylvania—it made old time group business meetings look peaceful and serene. The local Intergroup Association needed a treasurer and the Chairman of the Intergroup knew I had worked in accounting and control for many years so he suggested I should stand for the position. I did, and I was chosen. I knew all the Steering Committee members, and I showed up for my job, figuring this was another way to be giving back. And things went along for a while with no problem until someone came in with a check for $4,000 from a social group made up of members of A.A., but which raised money by selling raffle tickets and dance tickets to non-A.A.'s. I pretty much couldn't believe it—everyone knew it was a firm tradition that we couldn't take money from outside A.A. The Treasurer's Report—for reasons unknown—came at the end of the meeting. The Steering Committee didn't want the money, but it was at the end of the meeting, and everyone wanted to go home, and I made the mistake of agreeing to bring the question up at the next meeting, even though a majority of the Steering Committee had said we couldn't take the money.

Unfortunately people from miles around came to the next Steering Committee meeting to try to persuade me to deposit that check—the social group had made money out of their event, and they wanted that money to go to A.A. They said they were members of A.A. and we could accept their money. I said it was a firm tradition that we are self-supporting through our own contributions, and money from raffle tickets and dances collected in that fashion wasn't our own contributions. Our "guests" screamed and stood on chairs and tables—they banged their shoes—and then with all this going on, the Steering Committee began to resign. One by one, then two by two, I saw people I had known as dedicated A.A.s walk off the Committee that night. I went home while the screaming was still going on, put my monthly statement on a computer disk, got all my hard-copy and disks arranged, and went down and tendered my own resignation at the next meeting. You see, when the unity of A.A. is fractured, it's bad for the fracture to continue, and if one side isn't going to give way, the other must. The outcome may be bad—in this case it was, I think—but a bad resolution breaks the unity of A.A. less than no resolution.

A new Steering Committee was chosen by the Intergroup representatives (only the secretary didn't resign—she figured she had to keep the records). The new Committee took the money and deposited it in the Intergroup account—and most of it is still there. Many of the groups stopped contributing—after all, the Intergroup had enough money. A few groups still won't contribute, even though that was eight years ago—and $3,200 of the $4,000 is still in the treasury.

You know, the old idea was that only a couple of new Steering Committee members would be chosen each year, so there would be continuity and knowledge and institutional memory. All gone after this. And since that time, people who go to the Intergroup meetings talk about needing to wear armor, and talk about shouting matches month after month—even lack of a quorum month after month. I can't say whether these stories are true—I haven't been there—but they're widely told.

Fortunately that's not the only Intergroup Association I ever had experience with. The first Intergroup I experienced was a pleasure to work with and be with. When I was sober about five years there was a movement in our area to form a suburban intergroup association—the main intergroup was five counties wide, including one of the largest cities in the country— and the thinking was it was responsible for just too big an area to be of service to the people out on the edges in the farther suburbs. This move- ment was headed by my brother (he was then 32 and four years sober) and a man in his mid-forties (who had been sober a longer time) who later became my third husband. When they asked me to support them and work with them, I agreed.

At the meeting of people interested in this new suburban intergroup there was a large attendance—people were really concerned about the city intergroup operating so sketchily in the suburbs. Twelfth Step calls weren't getting through—we might not get the call till a week after it came in to the Intergroup—literature orders took forever—book orders took even longer. And besides that, if you had to go in to the Intergroup to pick up an order, it was all the way down in the center of the city, not in the best neighborhood, and some of the women wouldn't go there. If we had an intergroup in the suburbs, Twelfth Step calls would get through, and liter- ature and books would be available.

The last person to get up and speak was the president of our city Intergroup Steering Committee. He said, "I wish I could say you were all wrong but I can't—I know a lot of these things are true—we don't have enough hands to go around—we put out calls for help and they go unheeded—please understand, we really do need your help. So instead of staying up here in the suburbs, come down and help us—you can't imag- ine how glad we'll be to see you."

What he said struck a chord with me, so I showed up at the next inter- group meeting,—they were so glad to see me that I was instantly put on a committee chaired by a man named Bill J.—it was called the Unity Committee—I didn't know what it did and I said so—but they said "Just stick with Bill"—so I did. It was a small committee: Bill, a gal who was the assistant director, myself, and one other gal.

The next month the assistant director resigned and Bill asked for a vol- unteer. The two of us both volunteered. Bill reached into his pocket, pulled out a quarter and said, "We'll let God decide." I called it heads—it was heads—so I became the Assistant Director of Unity. This Unity Committee was mandated to contact every single one of the 500 groups in the five-county area once every two years, and this was the year. We contacted them by telephone or personal visit, where we booked what was known as a "unity pitch" meeting: we went to the group's regularly scheduled meeting, and the last half of the meeting, the Director of Unity chaired while all the members of the Intergroup Steering Committee were present—President, Vice President, Secretary, Treasurer, Director for Prisons, Director for Institutions, Literature Director, the secretary in the office—all were there to make a brief statement of what they did, and when they were all finished the meeting was opened up for questions.

This was unquestionably the most grueling job I ever had in A.A. We wrote flyers, copied them, distributed them—explaining about groups having anniversaries, new meetings, what committees did, the Traditions—it was an incredible opportunity—it was a great education, and when my double term (as assistant director, then director) expired, I missed it all terribly. It was work, hard work, good work, and there I learned that the more I gave, the more I got. And everyone who went on those unity pitches got a lot.

That was the year I became ill with thyroid cancer, and I was having difficulty driving and sometimes even walking—I had two radioactive treatments—they seemed to be going all right, but there was fear and more fear in me. I went to my doctor, who like all my doctors knew I was in A.A. (my sponsor Kay had made sure I told my doctors). I told him about my heavy schedule and asked him if I should resign. He said, "Miss S—, it would be a great mistake if you resigned or even cut back on your work in A.A." He thought my work was why I was making such good progress in my cancer treatment—I wasn't "sitting home in a rocking chair" all wrapped up in myself. He said he wished he had more patients with A.A. or something like it: "Patients' worlds can get awful small, so you just keep yours the way it is." So I did, and I did recover from the thyroid cancer, and I strengthened physically and mentally—and looking back, I strengthened spiritually too, because of the experience with the Unity Committee—and I loved it.

Looking back, I can see how this time spent working with the Unity Committee in the 1970s played a kind of counterpoint to what happened on that other Intergroup steering committee in the 1990s.

Setting up the meeting room and making the coffee are the beginnings of service work for most members of A.A., now that there are very few smoking meetings and you don't have to wash the cups and saucers any more. But there's another line of higher level service work besides group service and intergroup service. I mentioned our group's GSR—General Service Representative. It isn't necessary here to go into the structure of the fellowship of Alcoholics Anonymous in any enormous detail—fortunately!—but to make sense of my story here, you may need to know that, since alcoholics don't do well with rules, Bill W. set up Twelve Traditions in place of rules to keep A.A. working, and he set up a "General Service" structure to keep the Traditions working. Each group elects a General Service Representative, and the GSRs meet monthly in a District Committee. The District Committee elects a District Committee Member, who is really the Area (or State) Committee Member sent from that District. The DCMs meet (usually quarterly) as the Area Committee. Every two years the GSRs and DCMs meet in a General Assembly to elect a Delegate from the State or Area to attend the annual General Service Conference in New York. Questions about the Traditions and how well A.A. is working, and new literature, and corrections work, and work with the public and with institutions and professionals, are passed down the line from the Group to the GSR to the District to the DCM to the Area to the Delegate to the General Service Conference in New York to the A.A. Trustees, and then the answers come back up the line. The answers are never more than factual reports, or statements of past experience that could be considered suggestions.

I don't remember exactly when I served as a GSR for the first time (it was in the mid-1970s). It was in a district that's since been split and rearranged. But it had a DCM I will always remember and think of as "my DCM." He was born in Ireland and had a little bit of a brogue still, and he was sober almost ten years longer than I. As time went by, the people in the fellowship would say he came to look more and more like a leprechaun. He was strong on the Traditions. We would read the "Tradition of the

Month" every month—reading the First Tradition in January, and so on, down to the Twelfth Tradition in December—and we had a great long discussion as part of it—lengthy and loud. We took this all *very* seriously and we argued every Tradition as far as we could argue it, and we came to the conclusion that they were perfectly set up for alcoholics like us.

My DCM's name was Ambrose M., and he died while I was writing this book, so I never got to show it to him for his comments—but I had the advantage of knowing him and talking to him for more than thirty years. After our discussions, we all seemed to carry this knowledge we had gained of the traditions not only to our home groups but to any group we happened to be at. I can remember going through the announcements on the front table at a meeting to get them ready, and the next thing I knew, Johnny Q., who had been a GSR, went through those announcements and pulled out every one that didn't belong to A.A. We used to get a lot of flyers in those days about dinners and pig roasts and rehabs—and of course they weren't A.A. announcements—and he took them and crumpled them up in a little ball. I said, "What about my announcements?" and he said "They're not your announcements—they're not A.A. announcements at all!"—and they went into the wastebasket. Johnny was making the point that A.A. wasn't affiliated with these places or these events—we don't affiliate and we don't get involved in outside issues, which is Traditions Six and Ten.

I got a job working for a new rehab—I was very thrilled about it. I was the only woman working there and on a very nice salary. I had been there a few months when I realized they were using the A.A. World Directory for something—I didn't know what—and I asked about their using a document marked "Confidential—for A.A. business only." They told me they were using it for a big cocktail party for doctors to promote their place and they wanted some sober alcoholics in attendance, I asked if they had noticed the word "Confidential"—they blew me off—so I took it to a sober member who told me he would speak to the administrator.

He got the same response I got, but he said, "Don't worry about it, Janie—people who take that attitude toward A.A. don't last forever. You just sit back and watch!" He was right and within a couple of months they closed their doors. I don't know the connection between the two events, but I thought of this many years later (you see how you get to know the real significance of the events and pattern of your own story only in the process of telling it over and over, over a long period of time) when a non-alcoholic Trustee of A.A. in New York told me, "We don't go to law in A.A., we go to prayer."

After I "rotated out of service" as a GSR with my Irish DCM, I moved to another part of the state and had the opportunity to serve as a GSR there, a couple of times—for the most part a good experience—but in that district they refused to read the Traditions at the District Meeting. Sometime after that (five or six years) I became a GSR for a group in an adjacent district, and shortly after that I was elected Alternate DCM to replace a man who had resigned—I enjoyed that because the ADCM there visits the Intergroup to keep in touch with what's going on there—and in fact this district had two Intergroups, and neither was the one where I had been treasurer. I was asked sometimes about the Traditions, and how A.A. kept itself going. I got to see hardworking Intergroup members in action, it was easy service, and it was fun.

I had been ADCM for less than a year when the DCM resigned—he had taken it on under great duress because no one else would take it, and his sponsor said he should do it for himself and for A.A. Sometimes sponsors can be wrong—he took it on but it wasn't good for him or for A.A. He had been having more and more difficulty getting to the District meetings and he just wasn't himself. He decided to resign during our annual week-end Convention/Assembly in the Poconos, and spent some time with the Area officers. They tried to talk him out of resigning—they told him they would be in his corner if he needed help—but he came out of his corner and resigned that weekend, and I became DCM. I finished out his term and served a full term of my own after that, and except for a secretary who was having her own problems, and who resigned, everything was fine. We discussed the Tradition of the Month each month—around the circle of chairs we sat in—and we got a new secretary.

Most of the people were regular in attendance and my only real complaint as a DCM was having to sit in long, long meetings of the Area Committee, set at the four farthest corners of the fourth largest Area in the

United States—distributing reports *and then reading them aloud*, having to go through formal votes on matters that shouldn't have needed voting, too much pomp (I thought) and not enough circumstance.

But then, I wasn't running the meetings. I believe in General Service very sincerely: the GSRs and DCMs are the conduits from the groups to the area to the Trustees (and back again), and even if I think things aren't being done right, they're being done, and this kind of work keeps me in tune to what's going on in A.A.—and particularly what's happening in A.A. today, in addition to what happened years ago. I think it's a good system, and with the people I sponsor, I do the best I can to encourage them to be a GSR and go on if they can. I don't believe that "service keeps me sober," but I do believe that it keeps me vigilant—and by that I mean, after a long day at the office and a ride home full of traffic, and a household not all hunky-dory, I could easily convince myself to stay home and rest, but if I have a service commitment, somehow I can overcome all these irritants, and by the time I'm driving home from the meeting I feel better than I did before.

I'm also bi-polar—we'll get to that in Chapter VI—so I can fall into the pits of lowered thought, centered on "me myself" so very easily—but then I get to a meeting and my world expands, and I feel much better. Now this happens to me with other kinds of service too, but I think it takes place to a greater extent with this kind of service, where the Traditions and history of A.A. are brought to the surface.

The history part is important (and by the way, the Unity Committee on the Intergroup where I started out now has the local history and archives of A.A. as part of its responsibility). One thing that happens when you've been sober for "a few twenty-four hours" is that you have become something close to an "old timer" or "long-timer" and you get asked a lot of questions about the old days—so you become something like an A.A. historian. And in A.A., the closest service position to historian is Archivist or service on an Archives Committee. Bill W. said once that the archives of A.A. are in its members' stories, and it happened that when I was a DCM, I was chosen as a member and then as Secretary of the Area Archives Committee. Since that time I've been active in putting on (and co-chairing) our local multi-district History and Archives Gathering for the last few years, getting old-timers to tell their stories, and historian members of A.A. to share the results of their research. I've met a number of very enthusiastic A.A. historians and archivists. Their enthusiasm for A.A.'s history is something like the enthusiasm for A.A. itself I remember from thirty-five and thirty years ago. I'm not sure whether that's a good thing—but whether it is or not, it's certainly happening.

Before I was Secretary of the Area Archives Committee, I was a member of the Area *Grapevine* Committee. The *Grapevine* is A.A.'s monthly *Reader's Digest*-sized magazine, sometimes referred to as A.A.'s "meeting in print." This is one of the niftiest jobs there is in A.A. I went to functions all over Eastern Pennsylvania with a display of *Grapevine* magazines and all the other things the *Grapevine* puts out, such as tapes, videos, and books like Bill W.'s *Language of the Heart*. Everybody loves the *Grapevine*—it is very popular and very commonly read throughout A.A.—and eagerly read in prisons. Inmates love it. So at functions around the Eastern Pennsylvania Area I would set up a table with all the goodies sent to us from New York. I sold subscriptions to the *Grapevine* and to *La Viña*, the Spanish edition. We answered questions about other publications and about tapes, and talked to people about being *Grapevine* reps for their groups. It was a fun job, and I got to see a lot of people I knew but hadn't seen in a while—got to meet new people—and learned that A.A. had more publications than I knew about. I had a nice time doing that for my service work.

I was also nominated by our Area Delegate to serve as Appointed Committee Member, Trustees Corrections Committee, for four years, and it was one of the neatest experiences of my life. I wrote up a regular résumé and a résumé of my A.A. experience, and I was invited to interview for the position. I went up to New York for the interview, to 475 Riverside Drive, on a Friday in January. I was interviewed by the General Service Office Manager and the Chairman of the Trustees' Committee on Correctional Facilities (which was the name of that committee then) and the Secretary of the Trustees' Committee. Eventually I was approved by the Annual Conference as appointed to the Committee Member's position. This is a service position where I met with the full committee four weekends each year for four years.

My husband would drive me up to Manhattan on Friday afternoon— we would check into the hotel where the quarterly Trustees' meeting was held, have dinner (often walking over to the Oyster Bar at Grand Central), visit with some friends—and then Saturday morning at 10:00, I would be at the committee meeting, while my husband would head down to his favorite bookstore on Twelfth Street. After the meeting was a buffet lunch and General Sharing Session for the Trustees, Directors, and Appointed Committee Members. Then around 2:30, I would meet my husband and we'd have time together till the 7:00 dinner meeting, where he came as a guest. There would be three A.A. speakers at the dinner. On Sunday morning, we'd drive back to Pennsylvania.

In the committee meeting, we covered correctional facilities business for A.A. I served with another appointed committee member, a couple of directors, and alcoholic and non-alcoholic trustees. We reviewed literature being made available for prisoners, and videos that some of our committee members had made. Some of us were given speaking commitments around the country. I was working at the time for the Department of Corrections of the Commonwealth of Pennsylvania, and of course I had been going on commitments to prisons ever since my first year of sobriety, and I had my degree in Criminal Justice, so this was a perfect kind of assignment for me.

Serving on this committee was definitely a highlight for me. I met delightful and wonderful people, alcoholics and non-alcoholics alike. For me it was another opportunity to be proud to be a sober alcoholic and a member of the fellowship.

PART FIVE

SPONSORING OTHER WOMEN

And then—this isn't the same kind of "service" but it's at the core of Twelfth Step work—I have sponsored a number of women in A.A., well over a hundred, and I have made Twelfth Step calls for years. Sometimes it's very rewarding. Sometimes it's frustrating. You get a phone call—say it's patched through from the local intergroup or central service office—and "Mary" tells you she needs to go to a meeting—could you pick her up? She lives, let us say, at 452 River Road. Well, you get to 452 River Road, and it looks like it might be an alcoholic's house—at least one type of alcoholic. It isn't very well kept up, and the lawn looks like its chief purpose is maintaining a distance between the house and its neighbors. You go up to the door, and you hear steps going away on the other side, and then in a minute a man answers and tells you there's no one named Mary there. Well, there's nothing you can do, so you go away, but you know Mary was there, and she called you, but she got cold feet.

Every once in a while, Mary is there. Sometimes you wind up sponsoring Mary and she winds up sober. I had to learn the truth in the A.A. saying, "I was a successful sponsor—I stayed sober." Just so no one forgets, everything we do in A.A. we do gratis, for free—we don't charge for Twelfth-Step work. A number of years ago a gal named Ann and I went on a Twelfth-Step call to a woman in Conshohocken. We got there Sunday night. She was so grateful that we were there—two sober women who were willing to come out on a Sunday night just to see her and visit with her—we even went upstairs to her bedroom with her where she showed us where she used to hide her beer. She got her purse and got out her wallet and tried to give Ann and me money—of course we wouldn't take it, and couldn't take a dime from her or anyone else. We told her we went out on these cold wintry Sunday nights because we were grateful for what had been given us. She insisted and insisted—it was embarrassing—and we spent so much time with her that night we didn't get her to a meeting (we didn't accept her money either). But she got to her first meeting the next night—she met a young man in the program and married him and so far as I know they're both still sober. That's our "payment," if you like.

Like every other alcoholic, in one way or another I was Twelfth-Stepped, as I've mentioned, the night after my last drink—it was Tuesday, October 6th—I went to the meeting I had been to the year before, when I couldn't identify, and thought I would never return to an A.A. meeting again. That had been the meeting where the man suggested I try controlled drinking, and I did try it, though I never reached the point of any control at all. When I came back this Tuesday night a year later, I found I remembered some of the faces, and most of all I remembered this older woman, Kay H., who had been sober since about 1950. She and her husband had been friends of Bill W. and his wife Lois. I sat through the meeting ("sitting through" was what it was then) and after the meeting I went over to Kay and asked her to be my sponsor—she had been very ill, and in fact this was her first meeting in a while—she told me she didn't think she could be. I really begged her and another woman overheard me and came over and said "Oh Kay, be her sponsor!" So she finally said yes.

Kay told me what I had to do—not drink under any and all conditions—not take any mood-altering pills—be in touch with her and other women in the group—go to meetings, and once a week I had to go to a step meeting—"and don't give your phone number to men!" "But I don't understand." "You don't have to understand—just don't give your phone number to men!" I started out my sobriety with a sponsor who was really incredibly patient, who knew everything and really had a great sense of humor. I think she was a writer of medical reports and she had been widowed not long before. Her husband had been an engineer—they had traveled around the world after they got sober and she told me about the little cards that were always posted on the boats they traveled on, listing meetings of "Friends of Bill W." That was the first time I heard that expression.

I thought she was special then, and now I know she was. I wasn't a fan of A.A. meetings in those days, but I went because she said I had to. I thought that this business of everyone sitting around a big table and putting a dollar in the basket, and talking about their desire to be sober—I thought it was stupid and I didn't see how that kind of thing would help me. She told me it had worked for her and everyone else who had come to A.A.—I just had to let it happen. I put up obstacles at first—that was my way—but I learned from her that I had to stop putting up obstacles. The other women were very friendly, very nice, and they gave me their phone numbers when I asked for them—and there was no gossip (that I knew of). The men were very nice also, but my sponsor knew I needed to have positive friendships with women—not with men.

My first step meeting was Sunday afternoon, and the first one I went to was on the Third Step—it was down in the church basement, a small room next to the furnace room I think. We sat around in a circle with our Step books and I was very ashamed because I couldn't read the passages. I didn't know why it was—I'd always been a very good reader—I thought that maybe the fact I couldn't read came from years of alcoholic drinking, Valium, and double-hemisphere electric shock treatments. I was terrified that the damage was permanent. There was a public service spot running on television back then featuring fried eggs—labeled "this is your brain on drugs"—it looked like my brain felt, and I just didn't know what to do. My sponsor told me though that with the tender loving care afforded us in A.A. the damage to my brain would probably be only temporary. I remained terrified, thinking she was telling me that only to assuage my fears, not because it was true. I think now that there may have been some permanent damage to my memory, mostly from the shock treatments, but for the most part my brain works now, even now after being hit with central nervous system vasculitis three years ago and losing most of my sight—waking up one morning unable to see or hear or move. But I have stayed sober these thirty-five years and more, and my memory has come back some, even after the vasculitis. I've known a lot of people who have come into the program with impairments, and provided they've stayed around, and stayed sober, they've come out all right. But it helps if they've started out with good sponsorship.

My relationship with my sponsor was loving and affectionate—she was old enough to be my mother, in fact, she was nearly ten years older than my mother—she had a lot of love to give and she gave it—that's very important. We had her over to the house for dinner—we had cookouts on the grill on the deck—and having her in my life filled a lot of gaps for me. I could call her on almost any subject.

Not all subjects though. As it happens I didn't feel I could call her with the difficulty I was having with my sex life, because she was so much older—there was another woman in my group closer to my age so I went to her and told her the difficulty I was having. When I went to this woman—she was Mary K.—she told me, above all, don't drink—you may think you want a drink to carry you back to your old vibrant sex life—but don't do it. Stay sober, go to meetings, and pray, and your problem will eventually be resolved. I thought that was the most ridiculous thing I'd heard—treating such a serious problem of a physical nature by *going to meetings!* So I went to a doctor, who hold me the same thing—"Time and recovery—getting back to physical, spiritual, and emotional health will take care of this in time." Two weeks later I still had the problem, so I didn't believe him either. I mean, *two weeks!* So I went to the wife of someone I had known—she was a psychiatrist whose husband had been an alcoholic. She told me the same thing—relax, don't drink, be active in A.A., pray, and in time that problem will take care of itself. I must have accepted what she said—in any case the problem was resolved.

The reason I tell this story here is this: the first person I went to wasn't my sponsor, but was a member of the program (she later took over as my sponsor after Kay died) and she said, in effect, "Don't drink and go to meetings." That's what a sponsor would say. I could have stopped right there but I guess I had to have it proven to me. Since that time I've known a lot of people, with a lot of problems, and I've had some myself, and most of these problems have been resolved by a course of action you could summarize as, "Don't drink—go to meetings—reach out to your Higher Power." Why meetings? We've talked about that before. My brother Ted used to say that every A.A. meeting increases our level of consciousness. I know that was right.

So when I've sponsored women (and it's best from my experience to have it women for women and men for men), I've tried to be for them as much as I can what Kay was for me—and what Mary K. was for me later on, and

Jane S., and Big Book Mary, and Gerry M. ("Mom Gerry"). Sometimes it's difficult. A woman new in the program asks me to be her sponsor, because her counselor at the Rehab told her she needed to get a sponsor. Her counselor was right, of course. So I agree to be her sponsor—or her "temporary sponsor," which is a Rehab term I think—and she calls her counselor to tell her she's followed her advice, and then she wants to talk to the *counselor* about her problems. But the way it works, she'll have to begin talking to her *sponsor*, if she wants to start making real progress, and this would be a good time to start. There was one woman I sponsored for a while who couldn't get over the "wonderful experience" she had at her rehab—she went to "alumni" functions and talked more to fellow alumni than to anyone she met in A.A. She eventually felt she needed a sponsor more tuned in to her wavelength, apparently, and she found a new sponsor.

I remember a woman in New Jersey who called me often but before I was sober long enough to be her sponsor—she wouldn't get a sponsor and she used to call me and we would talk about things—but she didn't want a sponsor and she didn't want to go to many meetings. Did I learn from her? Yes. One day she called me and she was frantic—she had bought a bottle of whiskey—it was on the counter in the kitchen and she didn't know what to do. I said, "Throw it away!" but she was afraid to touch it and "would I please come over and throw it out?" I drove over and she was right: there *was* a bottle on the counter—I took it home to my house (I wanted to get out of there) and when I got home I didn't know exactly what to do—I put it on the counter and figured, I'll ask my husband when he comes home. When he came home, he took one look and there was the bottle and he thought maybe I'd been drinking—I said "No, I really just didn't know what to do with it," and I told him the story. He took the bottle and did something with it—I didn't care what, but I think he may have taken it to his uncle's house.

I sponsored a couple of women in my first few years of sobriety—but I don't think I was sufficiently involved in it. When I was sober four years, I was asked to sponsor a woman who I thought was a lesbian—I said I didn't know how to sponsor a lesbian—she said "Look, Jane, I'm not asking you to sponsor me on my sex life—I'm asking you to sponsor me in A.A.

for my problems with alcohol!" I needed that. I couldn't turn her down and I sponsored her for fourteen years and though we went our separate ways when I moved, we're still in touch, and we're both still sober.

Another woman I sponsored about that time told *me* what *we* were going to do—it was pretty difficult and maybe I should have told her to hit the road. We did the first three steps—no real problems. Then we got to the Fourth Step, where her inventory consisted of seventeen personality assets and no personality liabilities. I said I didn't think this was possible, we're all pretty much mixed good and bad. She said, "But I've gone over this thoroughly and I don't have any defects." I told her to take it home, reread the Big Book, and do a grudge list (list of people she had a grudge against and why), and she left. When I saw her a few days later she said she still had the same results. No liabilities, no defects. Now I knew she had to have defects—she was demonstrating at least one of them right there—but I didn't want to be the one to tell her. I think we had three visits with this still up in the air, and then she got a second sponsor who told her she was right, that she didn't have any liabilities—no defects—so there we were. But she eventually came back to me as a sponsor, we have remained friends, and she's sober thirty-one years now—she must have realized that, even if she didn't call them liabilities or defects or flaws, there was something not quite right.

The next woman I sponsored was Mary, who was the girlfriend of a member—she came into the program, loved the meetings, called me regularly, even gave us the name for our TLC ("Tender Loving Care") group—then one day she called me and told me she wasn't coming back—"I've thought it over and I don't think I'm an alcoholic." After two years of coming to meetings!

Then I had a call from a woman who said, "You don't know who I am, but someone else gave me your phone number—I can't get sober—I can't get sober—it won't work for me!" "Are you getting to meetings?" "Yes!" (But she wasn't getting to very many.) "I just want to drink all the time." I asked her, "What is going on in your life that you can't stop drinking? You have to get to meetings on a regular basis." She said, "I can't do that." I said "Why not?" She said, "I work the street." I had to take that home and digest it and I asked my sponsor about it—that was Big Book Mary at that time—and when Terry called me again, I said, "You know, Terry, you've got to get a regular job so you can get to meetings on a regular basis— punch in, punch out, so that somewhere there's a meeting you can get to on Monday, on Tuesday, each day." "My kind of work you don't have that." "Then you'll have to get another line of work if you want to be sober." I explained to her that we have to become willing to go to any lengths to be sober, and the next thing I knew she had a job working in an adult book store, with regular hours (although going pretty late at night), and before we knew it she was going to meetings on a fairly regular basis. It worked like a charm. She started to learn how to be sober. It took time for a complete break from her old life, but once she did she went to college and became a social worker and got a master's degree.

Over the years, I must have sponsored in the hundreds of women, and some have been a pleasure to work with (even though some of these didn't always stay sober), and some have been a pleasure because they stayed sober, but being their sponsor was sort of like taking medicine—it was good for me, and it worked, but it didn't taste good. And with some it simply didn't work out. One stole from my house. Another seems to have lied about her "other" diagnosis and then staged a fight to get out of the sponsorship relation—and I liked her a lot and still would, I know, if we were in touch. But even with heartaches, and even though I certainly made mistakes, I have been a successful sponsor. I haven't given up on sponsoring—I have never made the decision to give up on someone I was sponsoring—and I am still sober. The closest I have come to giving up was with a woman I had sponsored through more than a few "slips" and not a few jail terms. The fourth or fifth time she was in jail in a state a thousand miles away (and I was very ill) I told my husband to refuse a collect phone call from the jail—but I told him if she called back when I was better, and he answered, he should accept the call. But she never did, and I wonder if she thought I had finally given up. I wonder if she is even still alive. She has not called since that night, so far as I know, but I wonder sometimes when there's a call that comes in when I'm not home, and all that's recorded is that there was a call.

There's another kind of "sponsoring" in A.A., but it rarely happens. If someone who gets involved in general service work has a sponsor who hasn't been involved in it, then that person may need a "general service sponsor," usually called a service sponsor, to guide them through the business of GSRs and ADCMs and DCMs and Delegates and the GSO and the Conference, and the Area Committee and the officers on the Area Panel, and all that. My experience is that a person getting involved in general service work may sometimes be appointed a service sponsor (I've been one), but people who haven't already had a service sponsor appointed for them, figure out for themselves pretty quick that they need one. The service sponsor is there for emergency questions, or sometimes simply to talk "service" things over with every once in a while. There's nothing wrong with this, and sometimes it can be very helpful, but I don't think it really ought to be thought of as sponsorship—if anything, it's "advisorship."

This brings me to the third part of the Twelfth Step—practicing these principles in all our affairs. Practicing these principles in all our affairs is sometimes thought to be the hardest part of Step Twelve. Personally, I think we become involved in this part of the Step before we know we are. A lot of it is a matter of developing new habits of courtesy, of putting others ahead of us, of sharing whatever we have—whether it's time, information, hamburger or old copies of the *Grapevine,* whether it's picking somebody up and giving them a ride to a meeting, taking a meeting into a prison or the state hospital, or taking someone to the hospital or to a funeral—these are things we find ourselves doing along the way in our sobriety. They may not be in the Big Book and except for taking someone to a meeting they may not be talked about at an A.A. meeting, but I think they're within this part of the Twelfth Step.

There used to be a saying about taking what you learned at A.A. home with you—"if you don't have it at home, you don't have it." If you can't live with the people you live with, then you better get some more practice in the program. When I got sober I didn't get along with much of anyone—it was said of me that my motto was, "I'd rather be right than President"—or maybe just, "I *am* right!" I was naive enough to think that having all that information I had at my fingertips would impress everyone—I was wrong!

People resent know-it-alls. Next to not picking up a drink, that may be the hardest thing I had to learn. The other thing was, I thought that being a perfectionist was the way to go and people would be glad to know someone who strove so earnestly for perfection—I was wrong! I'm not a perfectionist any more (at least not to the degree I was) and most of the time I let other people take the reins and I hold back. I have to do this everywhere—in my job, in the fellowship and at home—perfectionism and "knowing it all" were defense mechanisms I had for not taking a real serious look at myself, because once I did take a real serious look at myself, these attitudes weren't any more attractive to me than they were to my associates and my family. Once in a while I still fall into some old habits and I have to remember that these flaws are being removed, yes, but not in my time and not in my way. But I hope the principles I'm practicing in all my affairs are love and service—this is my prayer.

CHAPTER VI

Questions on the Manic-Depressive (Bi-Polar) Alcoholic

In "The Doctor's Opinion" in the front of the Big Book of Alcoholics Anonymous, Dr. Silkworth mentions the "whole chapter" that could be written (presumably by a qualified doctor or at least by an alcoholic with a better than ordinary understanding of medicine), about the "manic-depressive" (now generally called the bi-polar) alcoholic. As I said earlier, this isn't that chapter. What I'm writing is based pretty much only on my own case, and my discussion of treatment is based pretty much only on my own treatment. But from my thirty-five years experience with alcoholism (my own and others) I am convinced there is misunderstanding of the "co-morbid" condition of alcoholism with manic depression, and too ready diagnosis of manic depression, and too early treatment for the condition among alcoholics.

I had a number of hospitalizations before I got sober, two after, and none after the hospitalization that came at the end of my second year of sobriety. I attribute my sobriety to A.A., and my absence from hospitals and day-clinics (since that last hospitalization) to lithium carbonate and a very knowledgeable physician.

But the three-month hospitalization in 1972 was pretty bad. I lost weight. I had tremors even without the medication which I had previously blamed for my tremors. I had visual and auditory hallucinations, even though I was sober and drug-free, and I started falling down. My husband somehow found a doctor who would take my case. By the time we reached

129

the hospital I was unconscious, and I remained unconscious for a week. I was kept in a side room by myself, in bed with a Posey strap. When I finally came to, I did not know who I was and where I was, and although I hadn't had any drugs, they couldn't be sure of that and were afraid to give me any. I was catatonic. I had to be fed, and at first the only thing I would eat was yogurt. I thought everything but yogurt had ground glass in it.

I was strapped in bed in the middle of the room, and had hallucinations that my head was disconnected from my body and bouncing around and hitting things. The window was barred and the door of the room was barred, and from my bed I couldn't see anything outside the room. But I found out later that there was sometimes a volleyball game going on outside, and I think I heard the volleyball bouncing, and being served or hit during the game, and the sound of the ball bouncing was what translated to my head bouncing around the room.

The hospital was an expensive place: we had waiters in the dining room (when I was finally allowed to go there) and the patients were allowed to request second helpings. There was one nice nurse—I later found out she was a stone alcoholic—but the rest were not nice. What redeemed the whole situation, and began my way back from the depths of my manic depressive psychosis, were the doctors, and especially Dr. Carlos Zarate. He was an Argentinian who had practiced in Europe, and I think he knew more about lithium therapy than any other doctor then in the United States, at a time when lithium therapy was out of favor here. I remained at Eugenia under his care from July 3, 1972, to October 5, 1972, when I told him "You have to let me out—it's my second anniversary" and he let me out.

It was Dr. Zarate who told me I would need lithium for my manic depression, and A.A. meetings for my alcoholism—a combined therapy, one day at a time—for the rest of my life. While I was in Eugenia, the first thing I was able to read was the Big Book. That was when I really held on to the Second Step—I knew I really needed God's help to be sane, and Dr. Zarate told me where the help would come from. It was in the hospital that I began the practice of doing a regular daily meditation using the little black book, *Twenty-Four Hours A Day*. I've already mentioned that book, which may still be the most-used book of meditations within Alcoholics Anonymous (although it is not officially conference-approved literature printed by Alcoholics Anonymous World Services in New York). When I started, I knew I was supposed to be reading it in the morning, but I couldn't manage it in the morning so I read it at night and didn't tell anyone. At night I couldn't decide whether I should read the reading for that morning or the next morning, so I read both. Eventually I managed to read it one day at a time, in the morning, as I was meant to.

During my three months there, Dr. Zarate began trying to introduce the lithium into my system very gradually. He told the nurses to put it in my cereal first. My tremors were so bad though, the cereal would fly off my spoon. They found they couldn't keep an accurate record of how much lithium was actually getting into my system, but it didn't look like much. Finally after several days Dr. Zarate came up with a new method to get the lithium into my system—the nurses put it on crackers with peanut butter. A nurse came in the afternoon with a plate with a number of crackers pretty well covered with peanut butter. I started eating the peanut butter and crackers—couldn't understand what it was about—they said, "Just take it—the doctor said so." I can say the tremors stopped with the peanut butter. I don't know how long the "peanut butter therapy" went on—perhaps a few days, perhaps a few weeks. I do know I wasn't on peanut butter when I left the hospital, so I think the peanut butter was used simply for the early introductory period for the medicine. But it worked like a charm.

Something that was very early impressed on me right after I got out of the hospital, was that people like me who have a serious mental illness need A.A. and all it offers twice as much as a plain alcoholic would. I was told I needed the socialization I got in A.A.—I needed a spiritual life that I would get in A.A.—and Dr. Zarate also told me I needed to be free of alcohol every day of my life, because if I ever drank again the results could be truly catastrophic for me as manic depressive, as well as for me as alcoholic. He told me I needed to have the interest of the service activities—an interest in something outside myself that challenged me as far as getting along with others, that challenged me mentally, and that kept me on the go physically. One of the unhealthiest things for me would be lethargy.

In my particular case he told me I should not be in a situation where I would sweat—like on the beach all day, which was my old habit—to drink gallons of water to flush the lithium salts from my system—to add a little bit of extra salt to my table food (not anything of a big deal)—and since I had so much difficulty sleeping I was to take the last lithium of the day between 5 and 6 p.m. The other doses I was to take at the same time every day, first when I got up (with breakfast, I wasn't to take them on an empty stomach) and then at lunch. I had to go to a lab for lithium levels to be taken on a frequent basis—the levels were to be given to Dr. Zarate to show I was taking my lithium as prescribed, eating as prescribed, and doing all the other things I was supposed to do.

Initially I despised this doctor—I was so sick I really didn't like anybody, but I particularly didn't like him. But as I got better—as I was doing exactly what he told me, and I began to see he knew what he was talking about—I finally decided he was the greatest thing since Dewar's White Label Scotch Whisky—in fact, for me now, he was much better than Dewar's White Label, and one super physician. For quite a number of years now I have followed—I'm still following in 2006—all the directions Dr. Zarate gave me in 1972—and I have never been hospitalized, unconscious, in a strait-jacket, or out of my mind. And as I have been sober longer and longer, somehow alcoholic women with this manic-depressive or bi-polar condition have been given my number, and they have called me and we have spent a lot of time together. It concerns me that a lot of manic depressive alcoholics—and even non-alcoholics—don't do well. I wonder if it's the fault of the poor information they get from their physicians.

I have sponsored women whose physicians gave them other (even inappropriate) medications on top of the lithium, and physicians who didn't require regular lithium levels. You know, when I became sober, I wanted to know everything there was to know about alcoholism, about being an alcoholic, about what you did about being an alcoholic—I had the disease of alcoholism and I wanted to know what to do about my incurable disease. I wanted to make sure alcoholism wasn't what got me. After 1972, I also wanted to make sure manic depression wasn't what got me, so I wanted to learn everything I could about manic depression.

So when I found out I was a manic depressive, I took the same tack I had taken with alcoholism. First I denied it—but when the denial stopped, I tried to find out everything I could about the psychology of manic depression and the lithium carbonate—for the simple reason that I wanted to get it right. I didn't want to sabotage myself. I would like to see more alcoholics and more people with mental illness adopt these behaviors on their own behalf, to protect themselves. I think there would be more success stories if the people who came into A.A. did everything they were told to do, and the same is true for the illness of manic depression. I have had a few very special friends who were both alcoholics and manic depressives, who have taken their own lives because of manic depression—I would give almost anything if they were here now.

Now, I'm still not a doctor. I wasn't a doctor when I started to learn about alcoholism and I wasn't a doctor when I started to learn about manic depression, and I'm not a doctor now. But over the years I've learned enough to know that there is sometimes a connection—perhaps more than one connection—between the two diseases. (Actually, Dr. Kay Redfield Jamison has estimated that 60 percent of manic depressives are alcoholic drinkers.) I think I understand enough about both diseases, even from my own experience, to know that both have to do with neurotransmission, that they have some characteristics in common, and that there is a kind of alcoholism that very often is connected to manic depression. A recent book calls it Secondary Depressive Alcoholism—*secondary* because the alcoholism often develops *from* the depressive condition.

I asked more than one physician why I didn't know I was a manic depressive until 1972 (even with being in mental hospitals), and they told me that alcoholism and alcohol masked the illness. When I was sober eleven months I went to a doctor in New Jersey who diagnosed me as manic depressive and I couldn't accept it—I told him I was just having trouble with my early sobriety, I was recovering from alcoholism, I was in the early stages of recovery—and I certainly didn't appreciate his diagnosis. He told me I had to take lithium every day. My husband told me I had to take it. The tremors were horrible—other medicine was added—the tremors were still horrible—and I finally left the hospital against medical advice. But before I left he told me it would get worse. I had no intention of letting it get worse—but it got worse.

What was important here was my complete denial of anything but alcoholism. But the situation did get worse, and eventually I couldn't continue to deny it. The other thing of course had been the tremors which I got from the lithium the way he was administering it to me, which I hated, and with no prescription of peanut butter from him. But the most important thing was, the first time around, I totally disbelieved the doctor who told me I was manic depressive and who told me it would get worse, but he was right on both counts.

What he didn't tell me, and I still don't know, is why I was a manic depressive. Was it because I was beaten in early childhood? Because of a childhood injury? Because of an inherited predisposition? I still don't know.

Very often one behavior of manic depressive patients is to disregard or completely discard their instructions (about taking the medicine, taking it at prescribed tines, and eating at prescribed times), while others seem never to have had the instructions. I had them, and I followed them, and am still following them, and that's another case where I don't know why. Unless that too is the Grace of God.

Prayer

My prayer is that in reading this book you will discover some of the answers to this baffling disease of alcoholism. I hope that you or the one you love will find what I have found—a life free of alcohol.

Love,
Jane

Elizabethtown, Pennsylvania
December 2005

978-0-595-42334-7
0-595-42334-5